Suzanna M. Rose
Editor

Lesbian Love and Relationships

Lesbian Love and Relationships has been co-published simultaneously as *Journal of Lesbian Studies*, Volume 6, Number 1 2002.

Pre-publication
REVIEWS,
COMMENTARIES,
EVALUATIONS . . .

"**G**ROUNDBREAKING in its emphasis on empirical research as the basis for understanding lesbian dating, courtship, sexual relations, identity, physical appearance, and friendships. CLEAR AND INFORMATIVE. . . . Should be read by all instructors of human sexuality. Researchers in sexuality and relationships will want to examine this book, and therapists who see lesbians will have to own it."

Maureen C. McHugh, PhD
National Coordinator,
Association for Women in Psychology

Harrington Park Press

Lesbian Love and Relationships

Lesbian Love and Relationships has been co-published simultaneously as *Journal of Lesbian Studies*, Volume 6, Number 1 2002.

The *Journal of Lesbian Studies* Monographic "Separates"

Below is a list of "separates," which in serials librarianship means a special issue simultaneously published as a special journal issue or double-issue *and* as a "separate" hardbound monograph. (This is a format which we also call a "DocuSerial.")

"Separates" are published because specialized libraries or professionals may wish to purchase a specific thematic issue by itself in a format which can be separately cataloged and shelved, as opposed to purchasing the journal on an on-going basis. Faculty members may also more easily consider a "separate" for classroom adoption.

"Separates" are carefully classified separately with the major book jobbers so that the journal tie-in can be noted on new book order slips to avoid duplicate purchasing.

You may wish to visit Haworth's website at . . .

http://www.HaworthPress.com

. . . to search our online catalog for complete tables of contents of these separates and related publications.

You may also call 1-800-HAWORTH (outside US/Canada: 607-722-5857), or Fax 1-800-895-0582 (outside US/Canada: 607-771-0012), or e-mail at:

getinfo@haworthpressinc.com

Lesbian Love and Relationships, edited by Suzanna M. Rose, PhD (Vol. 6, No. 1, 2002). *"Suzanna Rose's collection of 13 essays is well suited to prompting serious contemplation and discussion about lesbian lives and how they are–or are not–different from others. . . . Interesting and useful for debunking some myths, confirming others, and reaching out into new territories that were previously unexplored."* (Lisa Keen, BA, MFA, Senior Political Correspondent, Washington Blade)

Everyday Mutinies: Funding Lesbian Activism, edited by Nanette K. Gartrell, MD, and Esther D. Rothblum, PhD (Vol. 5, No. 3, 2001). *"Any lesbian who fears she'll never find the money, time, or support for her work can take heart from the resourcefulness and dogged determination of the contributors to this book. Not only do these inspiring stories provide practical tips on making dreams come true, they offer an informal history of lesbian political activism since World War II."* (Jane Futcher, MA, Reporter, Marin Independent Journal, *and author of* Crush, Dream Lover, *and* Promise Not to Tell)

Lesbian Studies in Aotearoa/New Zealand, edited by Alison J. Laurie (Vol. 5, No. 1/2, 2001). *These fascinating studies analyze topics ranging from the gender transgressions of women passing as men in order to work and marry as they wished to the effects of coming out on modern women's health.*

Lesbian Self-Writing: The Embodiment of Experience, edited by Lynda Hall (Vol. 4, No. 4, 2000). *"Probes the intersection of love for words and love for women. . . . Luminous, erotic, evocative."* (Beverly Burch, PhD, psychotherapist and author, Other Women: Lesbian/Bisexual Experience and Psychoanalytic Views of Women *and* On Intimate Terms: The Psychology of Difference in Lesbian Relationships)

'Romancing the Margins'? Lesbian Writing in the 1990s, edited by Gabriele Griffin, PhD (Vol. 4, No. 2, 2000). *Explores lesbian issues through the mediums of books, movies, and poetry and offers readers critical essays that examine current lesbian writing and discuss how recent movements have tried to remove racist and anti-gay themes from literature and movies.*

From Nowhere to Everywhere: Lesbian Geographies, edited by Gill Valentine, PhD (Vol. 4, No. 1, 2000). *"A significant and worthy contribution to the ever growing literature on sexuality and space. . . . A politically significant volume representing the first major collection on lesbian geographies. . . . I will make extensive use of this book in my courses on social and cultural geography and sexuality and space."* (Jon Binnie, PhD, Lecturer in Human Geography, Liverpool, John Moores University, United Kingdom)

Lesbians, Levis and Lipstick: The Meaning of Beauty in Our Lives, edited by Jeanine C. Cogan, PhD, and Joanie M. Erickson (Vol. 3, No. 4, 1999). *Explores lesbian beauty norms and the effects these norms have on lesbian women.*

Lesbian Sex Scandals: Sexual Practices, Identities, and Politics, edited by Dawn Atkins, MA (Vol. 3, No. 3, 1999). *"Grounded in material practices, this collection explores confrontation and coincidence among identity politics, 'scandalous' sexual practices, and queer theory and feminism. . . . It expands notions of lesbian identification and lesbian community." (Maria Pramaggiore, PhD, Assistant Professor, Film Studies, North Carolina State University, Raleigh)*

The Lesbian Polyamory Reader: Open Relationships, Non-Monogamy, and Casual Sex, edited by Marcia Munson and Judith P. Stelboum, PhD (Vol. 3, No. 1/2, 1999). *"Offers reasonable, logical, and persuasive explanations for a style of life I had not seriously considered before. . . . A terrific read." (Beverly Todd, Acquisitions Librarian, Estes Park Public Library, Estes Park, Colorado)*

Living "Difference": Lesbian Perspectives on Work and Family Life, edited by Gillian A. Dunne, PhD (Vol. 2, No. 4, 1998). *"A fascinating, groundbreaking collection. . . . Students and professionals in psychiatry, psychology, sociology, and anthropology will find this work extremely useful and thought provoking." (Nanette K. Gartrell, MD, Associate Clinical Professor of Psychiatry, University of California at San Francisco Medical School)*

Acts of Passion: Sexuality, Gender, and Performance, edited by Nina Rapi, MA, and Maya Chowdhry, MA (Vol. 2, No. 2/3, 1998). *"This significant and impressive publication draws together a diversity of positions, practices, and polemics in relation to postmodern lesbian performance and puts them firmly on the contemporary cultural map." (Lois Keidan, Director of Live Arts, Institute of Contemporary Arts, London, United Kingdom)*

Gateways to Improving Lesbian Health and Health Care: Opening Doors, edited by Christy M. Ponticelli, PhD (Vol. 2, No. 1, 1997). *"An unprecedented collection that goes to the source for powerful and poignant information on the state of lesbian health care." (Jocelyn C. White, MD, Assistant Professor of Medicine, Oregon Health Sciences University; Faculty, Portland Program in General Internal Medicine, Legacy Portland Hospitals, Portland, Oregon)*

Classics in Lesbian Studies, edited by Esther Rothblum, PhD (Vol. 1, No. 1, 1996). *"Brings together a collection of powerful chapters that cross disciplines and offer a broad vision of lesbian lives across race, age, and community." (Michele J. Eliason, PhD, Associate Professor, College of Nursing, The University of Iowa)*

Lesbian Love
and Relationships

Suzanna M. Rose, PhD
Editor

Lesbian Love and Relationships has been co-published simultaneously as *Journal of Lesbian Studies*, Volume 6, Number 1 2002.

Harrington Park Press
An Imprint of
The Haworth Press, Inc.
New York • London • Oxford

Published by

Harrington Park Press®, 10 Alice Street, Binghamton, NY 13904-1580 USA

Harrington Park Press® is an imprint of The Haworth Press, Inc., 10 Alice Street, Binghamton, NY 13904-1580 USA.

Lesbian Love and Relationships has been co-published simultaneously as *Journal of Lesbian Studies*, Volume 6, Number 1 2002.

The development, preparation, and publication of this work has been undertaken with great care. However, the publisher, employees, editors, and agents of The Haworth Press and all imprints of The Haworth Press, Inc., including The Haworth Medical Press® and The Pharmaceutical Products Press®, are not responsible for any errors contained herein or for consequences that may ensue from use of materials or information contained in this work. Opinions expressed by the author(s) are not necessarily those of The Haworth Press, Inc. With regard to case studies, identities and circumstances of individuals discussed herein have been changed to protect confidentiality. Any resemblance to actual persons, living or dead, is entirely coincidental.

Cover design by Jennifer M. Gaska

Library of Congress Cataloging-in-Publication Data

Lesbian love and relationships / Suzanna M. Rose, editor.
    p. cm.
    Co-published simultaneously as Journal of lesbian studies, v. 6, no. 1, 2002.
    Includes bibliographical references and index.
    ISBN 1-56023-264-1 (hard : alk. paper) – ISBN 1-56023-265-X (pbk. : alk. paper)
    1. Lesbianism. 2. Lesbians. I. Rose, Suzanna. II. Journal of lesbian studies.
HQ75.5 .L4423 2002
306.76'3–dc21

2002020546

Indexing, Abstracting & Website/Internet Coverage

This section provides you with a list of major indexing & abstracting services. That is to say, each service began covering this periodical during the year noted in the right column. Most Websites which are listed below have indicated that they will either post, disseminate, compile, archive, cite or alter their own Website users with research-based content from this work. (This list is as current as the copyright date of this publication.)

Abstracting, Website/Indexing Coverage . . . . Year When Coverage Began

- *Abstracts in Social Gerontology: Current Literature on Aging* 1997

- *BUBL Information Service, an Internet-based Information Service for the UK higher education community* <http://bubl.ac.uk/> 1997

- *CNPIEC Reference Guide: Chinese National Directory of Foreign Periodicals* 1997

- *Contemporary Women's Issues* 1998

- *e-psyche, LLC* <www.e-psyche.net> 2001

- *Family & Society Studies Worldwide* <www.nisc.com> 2001

- *Feminist Periodicals: A Current Listing of Contents.* 1997

- *FINDEX* <www.publist.com> 1999

- *Gay & Lesbian Abstracts* <www.nisc.com> 1997

- *GenderWatch* <www.slinfo.com> 1999

- *HOMODOK/"Relevant" Bibliographic database, Documentation Centre for Gay & Lesbian Studies, University of Amsterdam (selective printed abstracts in "Homologie" and bibliographic computer databases covering cultural, historical, social, and political aspects of gay & lesbian topics)* 1997

(continued)

- *IBZ International Bibliography of Periodical Literature*
  <www.saur.de> 2001
- *IGLSS Abstracts <www.iglss.org>* 2000
- *Index to Periodical Articles Related to Law* 1997
- *OCLC Public Affairs Information Service*
  <www.pais.org> 1997
- *Referativnyi Zhurnal (Abstracts Journal of*
  the All-Russian Institute of Scientific
  and Technical Information–in Russian) 1997
- *Social Services Abstracts <www.csa.com>* 1998
- *Sociological Abstracts (SA) <www.csa.com>* 1998
- *Studies on Women & Gender Abstracts <www.tandf.co.uk>* 1998
- *Women's Studies Index (indexed comprehensively)* 1997

Special Bibliographic Notes related to special journal issues (separates) and indexing/abstracting:

- indexing/abstracting services in this list will also cover material in any "separate" that is co-published simultaneously with Haworth's special thematic journal issue or DocuSerial. Indexing/abstracting usually covers material at the article/chapter level.
- monographic co-editions are intended for either non-subscribers or libraries which intend to purchase a second copy for their circulating collections.
- monographic co-editions are reported to all jobbers/wholesalers/approval plans. The source journal is listed as the "series" to assist the prevention of duplicate purchasing in the same manner utilized for books-in-series.
- to facilitate user/access services all indexing/abstracting services are encouraged to utilize the co-indexing entry note indicated at the bottom of the first page of each article/chapter/contribution.
- this is intended to assist a library user of any reference tool (whether print, electronic, online, or CD-ROM) to locate the monographic version if the library has purchased this version but not a subscription to the source journal.
- individual articles/chapters in any Haworth publication are also available through the Haworth Document Delivery Service (HDDS).

Lesbian Love and Relationships

CONTENTS

Introduction: Lesbian Love and Relationships   1
    Suzanna M. Rose

"Having a Girlfriend Without Knowing It": Intimate Friendships
    Among Adolescent Sexual-Minority Women   5
    Lisa M. Diamond

Against All Odds: The Dating Experiences
    of Adolescent Lesbian and Bisexual Women   17
    Diane E. Elze

The Impact of Group Membership on Lesbians'
    Physical Appearance   31
    Ilana D. Krakauer
    Suzanna M. Rose

Butch/Femme in the Personal Advertisements of Lesbians   45
    Christine A. Smith
    Shannon Stillman

Lesbians in Love: Why Some Relationships Endure
    and Others End   53
    Kristin P. Beals
    Emily A. Impett
    Letitia Anne Peplau

Not Any One Thing: The Complex Legacy of Social Class
    on African American Lesbian Relationships   65
    Ruth L. Hall
    Beverly Greene

A Butch Among the Belles   75
    Bonnie R. Strickland

Lesbian Dating and Courtship from Young Adulthood to Midlife   85
    Suzanna M. Rose
    Debra Zand

Beyond "Lesbian Bed Death": The Passion and Play
   in Lesbian Relationships   111
    Suzanne Iasenza

Lesbian Intimate Partner Violence: Prevalence and Dynamics   121
    Carolyn M. West

Couples Therapy for Lesbians: Understanding Merger
   and the Impact of Homophobia   129
    Maryka Biaggio
    Suz Coan
    Wendi Adams

Young Sexual Minority Women's Perceptions
   of Cross-Generational Friendships with Older Lesbians   139
    Jeanne L. Stanley

Building Bridges: Examining Lesbians' and Heterosexual
   Women's Close Friendships with Each Other   149
    Jacqueline S. Weinstock
    Lynne A. Bond

Index   163

ABOUT THE EDITOR

Suzanna M. Rose, PhD, is Director of Women's Studies and Professor of Psychology at Florida International University. She received her degree in 1979 from the University of Pittsburgh, where she first became involved with feminist psychology by team-teaching a course on the psychology of women. Her research focuses on how gender, sexual orientation, and race affect relationships and sexuality, as well as on general gay and lesbian issues.

Dr. Rose has published extensively on love scripts and friendship in professional journals, including the *Journal of Social Issues, Psychology of Women Quarterly,* the *Journal of Homosexuality, Violence Against Women,* and *American Behavioral Scientist.* She is co-author (with Barbara Winstead and Valerian Derlega) of *Gender and Close Relationships* (1997) and has edited two books on academic women's careers. She is currently on the editorial boards of *Psychology of Women Quarterly, Sex Roles, Women & Therapy,* and the American Psychological Association series *Contemporary Perspectives on Lesbian, Gay, and Bisexual Psychology.* In addition, she is a member of the grant review committee for the American Psychological Foundation's Wayne Placek Award, which funds research on lesbian and gay issues. In 1992, she received the Cheryl Ladd Frankin Award for contributions to feminist psychology from the Association for Women in Psychology (AWP). She also served as both Chair and Board Member or AWP for several years. Dr. Rose is a Fellow in the Society for the Psychology of Women and Division 44 of the American Psychological Association.

Introduction:
Lesbian Love and Relationships

Suzanna M. Rose

A new era of understanding concerning lesbian love and relationships is be-ginning. Lesbians now, at least occasionally, are portrayed as "normal" by the media. It might even be said that lesbians have "arrived" in terms of achieving a limited positive visibility within the larger culture. In the past decade or so, Ellen DeGeneres came out as a lesbian on her top-rated television comedy show and lesbians were featured on the covers of national magazines. Docu-mentaries dealt sympathetically with the topics of same-sex marriage, lesbian moms, and violence against lesbians and gays, such as the murders of Teena Brandon and Matthew Shepard. To some extent, lesbians even began to be per-ceived as having an advantage over heterosexuals in certain areas. For in-stance, in 2000, two authors published a book called *Lesbian sex secrets for men: What every man wants to know about making love to a woman and never asks* (Goddard & Brungardt, 2000). The book was advertised in men's fitness magazines and, apparently, sales were brisk.

Positive representations of lesbians, although still not the norm, are a wel-come shift away from the mental health model of homosexuality that domi-nated the twentieth century. The mental health model–or rather, the view that lesbianism was a mental illness–meant that research on lesbians focused pri-marily on one of two areas, either the causes of sexual orientation, or the psy-chological abnormality of lesbianism. A strong research tradition launched by Evelyn Hooker in the 1950s debunked the idea that homosexuality was a men-tal illness (Hooker, 1957). Later research showed that lesbians were quite sim-

[Haworth co-indexing entry note]: "Introduction: Lesbian Love and Relationships." Rose, Suzanna M. Co-published simultaneously in *Journal of Lesbian Studies* (Harrington Park Press, an imprint of The Haworth Press, Inc.) Vol. 6, No. 1, 2002, pp. 1-3; and: *Lesbian Love and Relationships* (ed: Suzanna M. Rose) Harrington Park Press, an imprint of The Haworth Press, Inc., 2002, pp. 1-3. Single or multiple copies of this article are available for a fee from The Haworth Document Delivery Service [1-800-HAWORTH, 9:00 a.m. - 5:00 p.m. (EST). E-mail address: getinfo@haworthpressinc.com].

1

ilar to heterosexual women in terms of psychological functioning, gender roles, sexual behavior, and relationship priorities (e.g., Thompson, McCandless, & Strickland, 1971; Peplau, 2001; Peplau & Garnets, 2000). This allowed new perspectives on lesbians to flourish. Instead of focusing on "why" a woman was a lesbian, sexual orientation began to be used in research in much the same way as gender. Lesbians, gay men, and heterosexuals alike were studied to see how both gender and sexual orientation affected relationship development and sexual behavior (e.g., Blumstein & Schwartz, 1983; Kurdek, 1994). These comparative studies sent a message that lesbianism was a sexual variation rather than a pathology.

What has not been fully accomplished, however, is an exploration of lesbian experience from the perspective of what lesbians view as important. Most current research on relationships contains embedded heterosexist biases that continue to guide what is asked and, subsequently, what is known about love, attraction, and mating (Rose, 2000). For instance, among heterosexuals, same-sex friendships tend to be defined as platonic relationships and researchers tend to ignore or deny other possibilities by not asking questions about sexual feelings. In contrast, lesbians often report that sexual desire arose within a deeply felt same-sex friendship. Thus, from a lesbian standpoint, the nature of sexuality within same-sex friendship would be an important area of study. The area of sexual signaling also plays out differently among lesbians than heterosexuals, but research on sexual attraction is dominated by justifications and explanations for heterosexual sexual displays (e.g., Buss, 1994; Kenrick & Trost, 1997). Heterosexual women use at least 52 nonverbal flirtation behaviors to signal their interest in men (e.g., skirt hike, hair toss, neck presentation) (Moore, 1985). These exaggerated feminine gestures do not seem to be utilized extensively by most lesbians. How then do lesbians discern sexual interest from another woman? This is an issue that routinely surfaces in commentaries and humorous descriptions of lesbian life, but about which we know little. A second aspect of lesbian experience that has been neglected concerns not what is unique but what is common to both heterosexual and lesbian relations. For instance, lesbians are not immune from problems such as intimate partner violence. Like heterosexuals, lesbians may seek therapy to help their relationships. These issues recently have begun to be addressed.

In this volume, original research explores what are compelling issues for many lesbians, including friendship, dating, butch-femme roles, staying together, sexuality, concerns of African-American lesbians, violence in relationships, and therapy. The assumption that lesbian relationships are natural and normal underlies our approach and reflects the new era of research on lesbians that has begun.

REFERENCES

Blumstein, P. W., & Schwartz, P. (1983). *American couples.* New York: William Morrow.

Buss, D. M. (1994). *The evolution of desire: Strategies of human mating.* New York: Basic Books.

Goddard, J., & Brungardt, K. (2000). *Lesbian sex secrets for men: What every man wants to know about making love to a woman and never asks.* New York: Plume.

Hooker, E. (1957). The adjustment of the male overt homosexual. *Journal of Projective Techniques, 21,* 18-31.

Kenrick, D. T., & Trost, M. R. (1997). Evolutionary approaches to relationships. In *Handbook of Personal Relationships* (2nd edition) (pp. 156-178). New York: John Wiley & Sons.

Kurdek L. A. (1994). The nature and correlates of relationship quality in gay, lesbian, and heterosexual cohabiting couples: A test of the individual difference, interdependence, and discrepancy models. In B. Greene & G. M. Herek (Eds.), *Psychological perspectives on lesbian and gay issues: Vol. 1. Lesbian and gay psychology: Theory, research, and clinical applications* (133-155). Thousand Oaks, CA: Sage.

Moore, M. M. (1985). Nonverbal courtship patterns in women: Context and consequences. *Ethology and Sociobiology, 6,* 237-247.

Peplau, L. A. (2001). Rethinking women's sexual orientation: An interdisciplinary relationship-focused approach. *Personal Relationships, 8,* 1-20.

Peplau, L. A., & Garnets, L. D. (Eds.). Women's sexualities: New perspectives on sexual orientation and gender. *Journal of Social Issues, 56,* 181-192.

Rose, S. (2000). Heterosexism and the study of women's romantic and friend relationships. *Journal of Social Issues, 56,* 315-328.

Thompson, N.L., McCandless, B.R., & Strickland, B.R. (1971). Personal adjustment of male and female homosexuals and heterosexuals. *Journals of Abnormal Psychology, 78,* 237-240.

"Having a Girlfriend Without Knowing It": Intimate Friendships Among Adolescent Sexual-Minority Women

Lisa M. Diamond

SUMMARY. This article provides a qualitative analysis of the intimate friendships of 80 adolescent and young adult sexual-minority women who were interviewed as part of an ongoing longitudinal study. Many reported having participated in a same-sex best friendship that they considered as committed, intimate, passionate, and intense as a romantic relationship. These "passionate friendships" typically combined components of the normative heterosexual friendship script with components of

Lisa M. Diamond is Assistant Professor of Psychology and Women's Studies at the University of Utah. She received her doctorate in Human Development from Cornell University. Dr. Diamond's research focuses on adolescent and young adult social and sexual development. She has written extensively on female sexual identity development, and has been conducting the first long-term, prospective study of sexual identity transitions among sexual-minority women. She also investigates how peer attachment relationships (particularly best friendships and romantic relationships) help adolescents and adults regulate negative emotions and physiological stress, and whether romantic relationships are uniquely beneficial in this regard. In this regard, she has been particularly interested in the phenomenon of "passionate friendships" among young women, i.e., intense bonds that straddle the boundary between friendship and romantic love.

Address correspondence to: Lisa M. Diamond, Department of Psychology, University of Utah, 390 South 1530 East, room 502, Salt Lake City, UT 84112 (E-mail: diamond@ psych.utah.edu).

[Haworth co-indexing entry note]: " 'Having a Girlfriend Without Knowing It': Intimate Friendships Among Adolescent Sexual-Minority Women." Diamond, Lisa M. Co-published simultaneously in *Journal of Lesbian Studies* (Harrington Park Press, an imprint of The Haworth Press, Inc.) Vol. 6, No. 1, 2002, pp. 5-16; and: *Lesbian Love and Relationships* (ed: Suzanna M. Rose) Harrington Park Press, an imprint of The Haworth Press, Inc., 2002, pp. 5-16. Single or multiple copies of this article are available for a fee from The Haworth Document Delivery Service [1-800-HAWORTH, 9:00 a.m. - 5:00 p.m. (EST). E-mail address: getinfo@haworthpressinc.com].

the normative romantic relationship script. For example, although passionate friendships rarely involved sexual contact, they frequently involved forms of physical intimacy (such as cuddling and hand-holding) that are usually considered exclusive to romantic relationships. Although such intense friendships are typically interpreted as unrequited love affairs, this misrepresents the unique nature of these bonds. Because such relationships challenge conventional notions about the distinctions between friendship and romance, as well as distinctions between heterosexual and sexual-minority women, they have important implications for understanding the interplay between emotional and sexual feelings in the close relationships of *all* women. *[Article copies available for a fee from The Haworth Document Delivery Service: 1-800-HAWORTH. E-mail address: <getinfo@haworthpressinc.com> Website: <http://www.HaworthPress.com> © 2002 by The Haworth Press, Inc. All rights reserved.]*

KEYWORDS. Lesbian, adolescence, friendship, romantic relationship, bisexual women, sexual minorities

INTRODUCTION

Friendships and romantic relationships loom large in most people's recollections of their adolescent years, and for good reason. These two types of relationships take on particular importance during the second decade of life. Researchers have found that youths become increasingly skilled at negotiating reciprocally intimate interactions as they mature, deepening and enriching their close friendships. When they eventually form romantic relationships that combine heightened emotional *and* physical intimacy, the results can be unusually intense.

Stereotypes and media images of adolescent girls' relationships reflect this view. Young women's same-sex friendships are portrayed as especially intense and important during the high school years, yet their first full-blown love affairs with men are supposedly more so. The assumption underlying this view is that although both friendships and romantic relationships may be emotionally intimate, the sexual "charge" of a romantic relationship gives rise to a heightened intensity that never emerges between platonic friends, no matter how close. Thus, friendships and romantic relationships are presumed to be fundamentally different types of social ties with correspondingly distinct spheres of affect and behavior.

Does this "separate spheres" model apply to *all* young women? Previous research has found that some sexual-minority women recall intense but platonic adolescent friendships containing many of the feelings and behaviors typically associated with romantic relationships (Diamond, 2000a). Although these "passionate friendships" might seem to challenge the separate spheres model, the conventional interpretation of such relationships is that they are not, in fact, platonic at all. Rather, they are reinterpreted as unrequited romantic relationships whose special intensity stems from repressed sexual longing.

The main problem with this tidy explanation is that the women describing such friendships frequently refute it. Although some sexual-minority women admit to having harbored secret sexual desires for their closest same-sex friends, others claim that the passion they felt for such friends was exclusively emotional (Diamond, 2000a). Clearly, the separate-spheres perception of platonic friendships as fundamentally distinct from and less intense than romantic relationships does not do justice to these unique relationships. Rather than reinterpreting passionate friendships as repressed romantic relationships in order to shoehorn them into the separate spheres model, we should carefully attend to sexual-minority women's own descriptions and interpretations of these bonds.

Toward this end, I present a qualitative investigation of the most intimate adolescent friendships of 80 adolescent and young adult sexual-minority women who were interviewed as part of a longitudinal study of female sexual identity development. Extensive detail on the methods and results of this ongoing research can be found elsewhere (Diamond, 1998, 2000a; 2000b). My aim here is to provide a more descriptive account of these women's adolescent relationships that highlights the challenges they pose for conventional interpretations of the links and distinctions between sexual and emotional intimacy. Finally, although a small proportion of these women developed passionate friendships with young men, I limit the current discussion to same-sex friendships (see Diamond, 2000a for a discussion of male-male and male-female passionate friendships).

BACKGROUND AND METHODS OF THE STUDY

Participants were 80 lesbian, bisexual, and "unlabeled" women between 18 and 25 years of age who were interviewed over the phone as part of an ongoing longitudinal study of female sexual identity development. Sampling took place across a wide range of settings, including (a) lesbian, gay, and bisexual community events (i.e., picnics, parades, social events) and youth groups in two moderately-sized cities and a number of smaller urban and rural communities in central New York state, (b) classes on gender and sexuality issues taught at a large, private university in central New York; and (c) lesbian, gay, and bisexual student groups at a large private university, a large public university, and a small, private, women's college in central New York. The recruitment strategy succeeded in sampling sizable numbers of bisexual women and nonheterosexual women who decline to label their sexual identity, both of which are underrepresented in most research on sexual minorities. However, the sample shares a chronic drawback with other samples of sexual minorities in that it comprises predominantly White, highly educated, middle to upper class individuals. Nearly all of the college-aged participants had enrolled in college at one point, and 75% came from families in which at least one parent had completed college. Sixty-three percent of women came from families in which at least one parent had a professional or technical occupation, and 84% were White.

I conducted scripted, 30-minute telephone interviews with each participant focusing on her most intense adolescent friendship. Participants were asked to describe the type and frequency of physical affection in the relationship, whether they became sexually attracted to the friend, whether the friendship ever involved sexual contact, whether they ever became preoccupied or fascinated with their friend, how frequently they spent time with their friend, and how important the friendship was–relative to their other close relationships at the time–as a source of support and emotional security. Finally, participants were asked to reflect on the specific similarities and differences between this friendship and typical romantic relationships.

CHARACTERISTICS OF SEXUAL-MINORITY WOMEN'S CLOSEST ADOLESCENT FRIENDSHIPS

It was like having a girlfriend without knowing it. We spent 100% of our time together–my other friends used to call her "the Queen" because they knew I wouldn't go anywhere without her. We used to sit on each other's laps, sleep in the same bed and stuff. Sometimes it freaked me out how intense it was, and the amount of physical closeness. My other friends said "Well, do you think about her sexually?" And I didn't, so they said "Then don't worry about it." I tried to go to college near her, but it didn't work out. When we said goodbye, I was crying so hard my whole body was shaking. We talked to each other on the phone every day that first year of college.

This young lesbian's narrative is typical of the descriptions these women provided of their closest adolescent friendships. Most notably, the emotional tenor of these relationships often resembled romantic love, a state described by

Leibowitz (1983) as involving feelings of excitement, desire for self-revelation and mutual understanding with the love object, fascination and preoccupation with the love object, possessiveness and idealization of the love object, and a sense that losing the love object would greatly diminish one's life. Many–and sometimes all–of these features emerged in women's descriptions of their adolescent passionate friendships.

For example, over three-fourths of women reported that they were strongly possessive of their friend's time and attention and chronically fascinated or preoccupied with their friend's behavior and appearance. As one woman noted, "I was always so tuned in to her–I would notice little things, like if her purse strap fell off her shoulder, and I would just quietly put it back." Another described her preoccupation with her friend as "borderline obsession," and described the type of continuous and intrusive thinking about the friend that characterizes the early stages of romantic infatuation (Tennov, 1979). Possessiveness was also common. Participants reported being oversensitive to the real or imagined threat of the friend's attachment to a boyfriend or to another close friend, and often sought reassurance that the friend continued to prize their friendship above all other bonds.

Given that such feelings and behaviors are so much more typical of romantic relationships than friendships, it is not surprising that women's friends and family members frequently misinterpreted their intense friendships as love affairs. As one young woman described,

> When I left for college she made me a goodbye tape of songs–love songs. A friend of mine found the tape and said "What guy made this for you?" It must have looked weird, because most people don't feel so strongly about their friends. But it didn't seem strange to me at the time–I did love her, that deeply. A day without her was unimaginable.

Perhaps the best example of how such relationships blurred the boundaries between friendship and romantic love is that of two friends who sought out a couples counselor to repair the tension in their relationship that developed during their first year of college-induced separation. At first, the counselor assumed they were a lesbian couple; after receiving a lengthy explanation of the depth and long history of the friendship, the counselor finally remarked, "I see–what you have is like a marriage, so that's how I'll treat it."

Physical affection was another common feature of these bonds. As one woman said, "We were always a lot closer, physically, than I was with my other friends. We would sometimes sleep together in my twin bed, sit on each other's laps–I didn't really do that with anybody else." Another noted that "We were so physical with each other that I feel like it made us more able to read each other's emotional cues . . . There just seemed to be a lot more massaging, back-rubs, playing with each other's hair, wrestling." Although physical affection is common in many young women's same-sex friendships, the *types* of affectionate behaviors that characterized these friendships–cuddling side-to-side, cuddling face-to-face, holding hands, gazing into each other's eyes–are particularly intimate behaviors that are usually only observed in parent/child relationships and romantic relationships (Hazan & Zeifman, 1994). Yet three-fifths of women reported routinely engaging in two or more of these behaviors with their friends.

Notably, participants often explicitly indicated that this affectionate contact was not sexually motivated. As one woman described, "It was like this pull to be *near* her, this longing for nearness, but it wasn't sexual." The distinction between affectionate and sexual motives for physical intimacy is obviously ambiguous, and thus, one might reasonably challenge these women's claims that such affectionate behaviors had no sexual overtones. Yet, it bears noting that by the time these women were interviewed, most had spent a number of years reflecting on these friendships and often actively searching their memories for evidence of repressed same-sex attractions. Although some succeeded in unearthing such memories, many others did not. In fact, some participants felt it was the *absence* of sexual attraction in the friendship that made them so comfortable with such a high degree of physical intimacy.

Some women, however, eventually became attracted to their friends, usually several years after the friendship had been established. Approximately half of the participants reported that at some point in the friendship, they experienced at least a fleeting moment of sexual desire for their friend. Yet notably, friendships that contained elements of sexual attraction did not contain higher levels of physical affection, possessiveness, preoccupation, or any of these "romantic" feelings and behaviors described above. This provides further evidence that the special intensity of these relationships is not simply subverted sexual interest.

THE DEVELOPMENTAL CONTEXT
OF PASSIONATE FRIENDSHIPS

Although women appear capable of forming such bonds throughout the life course (see especially Rothblum & Brehony, 1993; Weinstock & Rothblum, 1996), they may be particularly likely and uniquely meaningful for *young* women owing to the normative developmental tasks of adolescence. Specifically, peers become increasingly important as sources of support and security during this stage of life (Sullivan, 1953), and same-sex friendships play a critical role in this regard. Sullivan (1953) argued that close same-sex "chumships" are the first peer relationships in which true reciprocal intimacy becomes established, and research has found that young *women's* same-sex friendships are especially intimate and affectionate, both emotionally and physically (Barth & Kinder, 1988; Buhrmester & Furman, 1987; Bukowski, Gauze, Hoza, & Newcomb, 1993; Savin-Williams & Berndt, 1990; Stoneman, Brody, & MacKinnon, 1986).

Notably, the most intense friendships were described as occurring during early rather than late adolescence. This may be because youths who are less sexually mature are less likely than their older counterparts to perceive a necessary association between sexual and emotional intimacy. As one woman indicated,

> At that age–I was 14–we had no sense of what it looked like from the outside, we just thought that we were friends, like any friends. At some point, we became much more physically affectionate, and her mom found out and told us we couldn't see each other. We didn't even understand why. I didn't figure it out until years later. Maybe if we had been older, we would have thought that we either had to back off, or just turn it into a romantic relationship. But at that time, it never even occurred to us.

Furthermore, romantic relationships may begin to compete with passionate friendships for a woman's time and attention during late adolescence, making it difficult to sustain the unique intensity of these bonds. In this regard, it is important to note that most sexual-minority women's adolescent romantic relationships are exclusively heterosexual (Savin-Williams, 1996). Because sexual-minority women tend to experience their first same-sex attractions and to identify as lesbian or bisexual at later ages than their male counterparts (Boxer, Cook, & Herdt, 1989; Savin-Williams, 1990; Sears, 1991), they are less likely than young gay and bisexual men to pursue same-sex romances and more likely to engage in normative cross-sex relationships.

SEXUAL INVOLVEMENT WITH PASSIONATE FRIENDS

The few sexual-minority women that *do* manage to develop same-sex romantic relationships during the high school years frequently do so with friends (Savin-Williams & Diamond, in press; Vetere, 1983). Thus, the transformation of a passionate friendship into a sexual relationship is often a woman's first direct experience with same-sex sexuality. Such a relationship often initiates or accelerates a sexual-minority woman's process of sexual questioning and identification. However, not all women who become sexually involved with passionate friends eventually identify as lesbian or bisexual, even when they find this same-sex experience both emotionally and physically satisfying. This further highlights the importance of studying such friendships on their own terms, rather than interpreting them strictly as adolescent precursors to adult lesbian relationships.

Some participants reported experiencing unexpected, unprecedented same-sex attractions for passionate friends that seemed to emanate directly from the unique emotional intensity of the relationship. Some of these women never again experience same-sex attractions, suggesting that such attractions may sometimes represent emergent properties of intense affectional bonds rather than unequivocal "markers" of lesbian or bisexual orientations. This, of course, directly contradicts conventional models of sexual desire and orientation. As Blumstein and Schwartz (1990) noted, such models contend that it is impossible to experience "some" same-sex attractions for one specific individual.

Yet this is precisely what some women described. One notable case was a woman who had just begun questioning her sexual identity when I first interviewed her:

> Just last week I sort of became involved with my best friend, who I'm currently living with, and who I've known since I was 12. We've always been really affectionate, but last Tuesday it just sort of kept going. I stopped it at first–I was sort of freaked out. Finally we just let it happen. I don't know what we're doing–are we dating? We haven't even told anyone. Right now I only have these feelings for her, and I don't know if that'll change. I don't know if I'm a lesbian. I just know I want to be with her, forever.

At the second interview 2 years later, this young woman reported that her clandestine sexual relationship lasted for over a year, during which time neither partner experienced same-sex attractions for any other woman. They finally terminated their sexual involvement after disagreeing on whether to continue hiding the relationship, but continued to live together and to maintain a primary emotional relationship. As she said, "The sexual part is over, but that was never the main thing. She's still the most important person in my life."

Similarly, another respondent who became sexually involved with a passionate friend claimed that "It was like taking the relationship to the next level–in some ways, I guess it felt like the only way I could express how deeply I felt about her." These cases indicate that the *emergence* of sexual desire or activity within an adolescent's passionate friendship need not indicate that either of the participants is lesbian or bisexual, just as the *lack* of sexual desire or activity in the passionate friendships of sexual minorities need not indicate that either participant is denying the sexual nature of the relationship. For both sexual-minority and heterosexual adolescents, sexual desire and activity with passionate friends may be an unexpected consequence of the unusual emotional and physical intimacy of the relationship.

PASSIONATE FRIENDSHIPS AND SEXUAL IDENTITY

I do not, however, intend to suggest that a woman's same-sex sexuality has no bearing on her participation or behavior in same-sex passionate friendships. Although this study cannot speak to the overall prevalence of passionate friendships, it is reasonable to expect that they occur with greater frequency among sexual minorities than among heterosexuals. Yet, the basis for such an association is not as self-evident as it might first appear. As noted above, we cannot simply assume that such friendships are motivated by sexual-minority women's same-sex attractions. Furthermore, because *affectional* components of sexual orientation remain sorely under-researched (Brown, 1995), we do not yet understand the extent to which sexual orientation circumscribes individuals' motivations and capacities to bond emotionally with men and women at different stages of life.

This blind spot is particularly problematic given the fluidity between emotional and sexual feelings reported by many sexual-minority women. A large body of research demonstrates that strong affectional bonds between women often provide a critical foundation for experiences of same-sex sexual desire. Not only do sexual-minority women frequently experience their first same-sex attraction and first same-sex contact with close friends (Gramick, 1984; Kitzinger & Wilkinson, 1995; Savin-Williams & Diamond, in press; Vetere, 1983), but many continue to employ a "friendship script" in courting future lovers (Peplau & Amaro, 1982; Rose, Zand, & Cini, 1993). In fact, some sexual-minority women have trouble distinguishing between close, same-sex friendships and same-sex love affairs, given the primacy of emotional intimacy in both relationships (Rose et al., 1993).

How then might we conceptualize possible associations between sexual identity and participation in passionate friendships? One possibility is that this association is spurious, resulting from an unmeasured third variable: openness to physical and emotional intimacy with women. Such openness might facilitate strong same-sex attachments among *all* female adolescents, but may have the added effect of accelerating sexual questioning among sexual-minority women. Previous research has documented considerable variation in the ages at which sexual-minority women first experience same-sex attractions and adopt non-heterosexual identities. Some do so in early adolescence, whereas others do so in their 30s or 40s (Golden, 1996; Kitzinger & Wilkinson, 1995; Rust, 1992; 1993; Weinberg, Williams, & Pryor, 1994). The women in the current sample first questioned their sexual identities between 14 and 20 years of age. Given the salience of same-sex friendships for women's sexual questioning, it is plausible that female adolescents who are comfortable pursuing close, affectionate friendships with female friends will more quickly become aware of their same-sex attractions. These and other possibilities should be explored in future research. The key point is that knowing a young woman's eventual identity does not necessarily reveal her history of and motives for close contact with either female *or* male peers during adolescence.

CONCLUSION

Because both popular and scientific conceptions of interpersonal relationships assume consistent boundaries between friendship and romance, they offer only two possible characterizations of unusually intimate bonds between young women: unacknowledged and unconsummated same-sex romances or "just friends." Neither, however, effectively captures the distinctive nature of young sexual-minority women's most intimate adolescent friendships. While the former mistakenly conflates passion with explicit sexual arousal, the latter fails to communicate the unique importance of these relationships. As Rothblum (1997) noted, the label "friend" is conventionally applied to *any* individual with whom one is not sexually involved, thereby placing soulmates and casual acquaintances in the same category.

Overall, sexual-minority women's descriptions of their passionate friendships caution against assuming that (a) any female adolescent who eventually identifies as lesbian or bisexual must have been sexually attracted to any female friend with whom she shared an intense emotional bond; (b) friendships become emotionally passionate only when there is an undercurrent of sexual attraction; and (c) the emergence of sexual attraction for a passionate friend, or the initiation of sexual contact with a passionate friend, expresses and is delimited by a woman's sexual orientation. Instead, these women's experiences suggest that interconnections between passion, attraction, sexual activity, and sexual orientation are relatively fluid and situation-dependent. Bonds that violate the "separate spheres" conceptualization of friendships and romantic relationships are deserving of systematic study because they raise critical questions not only about what "qualifies" a relationship as romantic, intimate or emotionally primary, but what "qualifies" a woman as lesbian or bisexual. Addressing these issues is central to understanding the social and sexual development of sexual-minority *and* heterosexual women.

REFERENCES

Barth, R. J., & Kinder, B. N. (1988). A theoretical analysis of sex differences in same-sex friendships. *Sex Roles, 19*, 349-363.

Blumstein, P., & Schwartz, P. (1990). Intimate relationships and the creation of sexuality. In D. P. McWhirter, S. A. Sanders, & J. M. Reinisch (Eds.), *Homosexuality/heterosexuality: Concepts of sexual orientation* (pp. 307-320). New York: Oxford University Press.

Boxer, A. M., Cook, J. A., & Herdt, G. (1989). *First homosexual and heterosexual experiences reported by gay and lesbian youth in an urban community.* Paper presented at the Annual Meeting of the American Sociological Association, San Francisco, California.

Brown, L. (1995). Lesbian identities: Concepts and issues. In A. R. D'Augelli & C. Patterson (Eds.), *Lesbian, gay, and bisexual identities over the lifespan* (pp. 3-23). New York: Oxford University Press.

Buhrmester, D., & Furman, W. (1987). The development of companionship and intimacy. *Child Development, 58*, 1101-1113.

Bukowski, W., Gauze, C., Hoza, B., & Newcomb, A. F. (1993). Differences and consistency between same-sex and other-sex peer relationships during early adolescence. *Developmental Psychology, 29*, 255-263.

Diamond, L. M. (1998). Development of sexual orientation among adolescent and young adult women. *Developmental Psychology, 34*, 1085-1095.

Diamond, L. M. (2000a). Passionate friendships among adolescent sexual-minority women. *Journal of Research on Adolescence, 10*, 191-209.

Diamond, L. M. (2000b). Sexual identity, attractions, and behavior among young sexual-minority women over a two-year period. *Developmental Psychology, 36*, 241-250.

Golden, C. (1996). What's in a name? Sexual self-identification among women. In R. C. Savin-Williams & K. M. Cohen (Eds.), *The lives of lesbians, gays, and bisexuals: Children to adults* (pp. 229-249). Fort Worth, TX: Harcourt Brace.

Gramick, J. (1984). Developing a lesbian identity. In T. Darty & S. Potter (Eds.), *Women-identified women* (pp. 31-44). Palo Alto, CA: Mayfield.

Hazan, C., & Zeifman, D. (1994). Sex and the psychological tether. In D. Perlman & K. Bartholomew (Eds.), *Advances in personal relationships: A research annual* (Vol. 5, pp. 151-177). London: Jessica Kingsley Publishers.

Kitzinger, C., & Wilkinson, S. (1995). Transitions from heterosexuality to lesbianism: The discursive production of lesbian identities. *Developmental Psychology, 31*, 95-104.

Leibowitz, M. (1983). *The chemistry of love.* New York: Berkeley Books.

Peplau, L. A., & Amaro, H. (1982). Understanding lesbian relationships. In W. Paul, J. D. Weinrich, J. C. Gonsiorek, & M. E. Hotvedt (Eds.), *Homosexuality: Social, psychological, and biological issues* (pp. 233-248). Beverly Hills: Sage.

Rose, S., Zand, D., & Cini, M. A. (1993). Lesbian courtship scripts. In E. D. Rothblum & K. A. Brehony (Eds.), *Boston marriages* (pp. 70-85). Amherst: University of Massachusetts Press.

Rothblum, E. D. (1997). *Help! My friend is sexually attracted to me! In J. S. Weinstock (Chair), Lesbian friendships and social change. Symposium conducted at the annual meetings of the Association for Women in Psychology, Pittsburgh, PA.*

Rothblum, E. D., & Brehony, K. A. (Eds.). (1993). *Boston marriages.* Amherst: University of Massachusetts Press.

Rust, P. (1992). The politics of sexual identity: Sexual attraction and behavior among lesbian and bisexual women. *Social Problems, 39,* 366-386.

Rust, P. (1993). Coming out in the age of social constructionism: Sexual identity formation among lesbians and bisexual women. *Gender and Society, 7,* 50-77.

Savin-Williams, R. C. (1990). *Gay and lesbian youth: Expressions of identity.* Washington, DC: Hemisphere.

Savin-Williams, R. C. (1996). Dating and romantic relationships among gay, lesbian, and bisexual youths, *The lives of lesbians, gays, and bisexuals: Children to adults* (pp. 166-180). Fort Worth, TX: Harcourt Brace.

Savin-Williams, R. C., & Berndt, T. J. (1990). Friendship and peer relations. In S. S. Feldman & G. R. Elliott (Eds.), *At the threshold: The developing adolescent* (pp. 277-307). Cambridge, MA: Harvard University Press.

Savin-Williams, R. C., & Diamond, L. M. (2000). Sexual identity trajectories among sexual-minority youths: Gender comparisons. *Archives of Sexual Behavior, 29,* 419-440.

Sears, J. T. (1991). *Growing up gay in the South: Race, gender, and journeys of the spirit.* New York: Harrington Park Press.

Stoneman, Z., Brody, G. H., & MacKinnon, C. E. (1986). Same-sex and cross-sex siblings: Activity choices, roles, behaviors, and gender stereotypes. *Sex Roles, 9/10,* 495-511.

Sullivan, H. S. (1953). *The interpersonal theory of psychiatry.* New York: Norton.

Tennov, D. (1979). *Love and limerence: The experience of being in love.* New York: Stein and Day.

Vetere, V. A. (1983). The role of friendship in the development and maintenance of lesbian love relationships. *Journal of Homosexuality, 8,* 51-65.

Weinberg, M. S., Williams, C. J., & Pryor, D. W. (1994). *Dual attraction: Understanding bisexuality.* New York: Oxford University Press.

Weinstock, J. S., & Rothblum, E. D. (Eds.). (1996). *Lesbian friendships: For ourselves and for each other.* New York: NYU Press.

Against All Odds:
The Dating Experiences
of Adolescent Lesbian and Bisexual Women

Diane E. Elze

SUMMARY. Research with gay, lesbian and bisexual adolescents has tended to focus on their psychosocial risk factors, with little attention paid to their dating experiences. Unique in its focus on younger, high school-age women, the present study examined dating relationships among 112 lesbian and bisexual women, ages 13 to 18. Characteristics of the young women's dating relationships were explored, as well as dating stress, the presence of verbal and physical abuse in their dating relationships, and psychosocial factors associated with dating. Findings indicate that, despite potential barriers, adolescent lesbian and bisexual women actively date. Relationship concerns requiring supportive interventions by youth-serving professionals are identified and study limitations are discussed. *[Article copies available for a fee from The Haworth Document Delivery Service: 1-800-HAWORTH. E-mail address:*

Diane E. Elze, PhD, is Assistant Professor at the George Warren Brown School of Social Work, Washington University, St. Louis. Her research interests focus on adolescent health and mental health, with a particular focus on gay, lesbian, bisexual and transgender youth; HIV prevention with adolescents; and the challenges facing HIV-positive adolescents related to treatment adherence.

Address correspondence to: Diane E. Elze, PhD, George Warren Brown School of Social Work, Campus Box 1196, Washington University, St. Louis, MO 63130 (E-mail: delze@gwbmail.wustl.edu).

This research was supported by grant no. RO3 MH58982-01 from the National Institute of Mental Health.

[Haworth co-indexing entry note]: "Against All Odds: The Dating Experiences of Adolescent Lesbian and Bisexual Women." Elze, Diane E. Co-published simultaneously in *Journal of Lesbian Studies* (Harrington Park Press, an imprint of The Haworth Press, Inc.) Vol. 6, No. 1, 2002, pp. 17-29; and: *Lesbian Love and Relationships* (ed: Suzanna M. Rose) Harrington Park Press, an imprint of The Haworth Press, Inc., 2002, pp. 17-29. Single or multiple copies of this article are available for a fee from The Haworth Document Delivery Service [1-800-HAWORTH, 9:00 a.m. - 5:00 p.m. (EST). E-mail address: getinfo@haworthpressinc.com].

<getinfo@haworthpressinc.com> Website: <http://www.haworthPress.com>
© 2002 by The Haworth Press, Inc. All rights reserved.]

KEYWORDS. Lesbian, bisexual women, sexual minorities, adolescence, dating, coming out

"Tell me about it!"
–written in the margin by a 16-year-old lesbian, next to a question asking about stress associated with trying to find people to date.

"That I'll always be alone."
–written by a 15-year-old lesbian, in response to the question, "Please describe any other concerns you have[about dating]."

The young women's words above echo the laments and fears of many lesbian and bisexual teenagers who face multiple barriers in exploring their emotional and erotic attractions. Adolescence is a time for young people to experiment with sexual and romantic feelings and relationships and to expand their awareness of emotionality (e.g., Savin-Williams & Berndt, 1990). The difficulty young lesbian and bisexual women experience in establishing romantic relationships is one of the many challenges they face as they attempt to construct their adolescent lives within social contexts frequently marked by stigmatization, victimization, isolation, and lack of support (Hetrick & Martin, 1987).

However, with a few important exceptions (Diamond, Savin-Williams, & Dube, 1999; Savin-Williams, 1990, 1996), little research has highlighted the importance of adolescent lesbian and bisexual women's experiences with dating and falling in love. Concerns about love and romance are often lost amid the necessary attention paid to sexual minority youth's experiences with victimization (Pilkington & D'Augelli, 1995), stigmatization (Martin & Hetrick, 1988), and their risks for HIV infection (Rotheram-Borus et al., 1994), substance use (Rosario, Hunter, & Gwadz, 1997), suicidality (Rotheram-Borus, Hunter, & Rosario, 1994) and other mental health problems (D'Augelli & Hershberger, 1993; Elze, 1999).

Dating and romantic relationships constitute important social contexts for adolescents' social and emotional development, providing young women with opportunities to explore intimacy and sexuality, rehearse romantic and sexual behaviors, enhance their social competence, and consolidate their identities (e.g., Furman, Brown, & Feiring, 1999; Neeman, Hubbard, & Masten, 1995). The social context of intimate relationships, however, is less available to many lesbian, gay, and bisexual adolescents. Unless community-based support groups or school-based gay-straight alliances exist in their communities, the pool of potential dating partners may be severely limited.

Well-founded fears of physical victimization, verbal harassment, peer rejection, and public humiliation further constrain the ability to seek out dating partners and romantic relationships (Savin-Williams, 1996). Although popular media bombards adolescents with cultural images of romance and love, sexual minority adolescents see few images of same-sex couples actively involved in romantic relationships. Given the cultural shroud that renders same-sex romances invisible, Herdt and Boxer (1993) suggested that same-sex dating is "an odd and perfectly unfamiliar idea" to young people with same-sex desires and attractions (p. 141). If, against all odds, sexual minority adolescents successfully date, the threat of negative repercussions often requires them to hide these relationships from peers, family members, and other significant adults, thereby depriving their relationships of public support and affirmation. Considering the barriers encountered by adolescent lesbian and bisexual women in establishing and maintaining romantic relationships, succeeding at same-sex dating is a testament to their resilience.

Few studies have explored dating and romantic relationships among high school age lesbian and bisexual women. Diamond's (2000) important contribution to the literature on sexual minority women's sexual identity, attractions, and behaviors sampled predominantly college-age young women, as did Savin-Williams' (1990) study on self-esteem and coming out among gay and lesbian youths. Existing research indicates the following: Many young lesbians and bisexual women experience same-sex romantic relationships (D'Augelli & Hershberger, 1993; Savin-Williams, 1990); involvement in same-sex romances is associated with greater openness about sexual orientation (Savin-Williams, 1990); and a friendship, dating or romantic relationship usually provides the context for their first same-sex sexual experience (Herdt & Boxer, 1993). In addition, most young lesbians date heterosexually during high school and report past or current sexual activity with males (e.g, Rosario et al., 1996).

Little is known, however, about how young lesbians and bisexual women compare on characteristics of their dating relationships, or about the potential risks and benefits associated with same-sex dating. Savin-Williams (1990) found that involvement in same-sex romances did not predict young women's self-esteem. Research suggests that suicidal ideation is significantly related to problems in romantic relationships (D'Augelli & Hershberger, 1993). Although the prevalence of dating violence among heterosexual adolescents is well-documented (e.g., Bennett & Fineran, 1998), no published research has examined dating violence among lesbian and bisexual female adolescents.

The purpose of this study was to add to the knowledge base on dating relationships among lesbian and bisexual women. The present research was unique in its focus on younger, high school-age lesbian and bisexual women. The specific questions addressed were: (a) What are the characteristics of lesbian and bisexual female adolescents' recent dating relationships? (b) To what extent do lesbian and bisexual female adolescents report dating-related stress (including suicidality) and violence? (c) What individual and social factors are associated with same-sex dating or involvement in a primary same-sex relationship for adolescent lesbians and bisexual women?

METHOD

Sample and Procedures

The present study was part of a larger investigation examining risk and protective factors related to gay, lesbian and bisexual adolescents' mental health and behavioral functioning. Self-identified lesbian, gay, and bisexual youths, ages 13 to 18, in northern New England, were recruited through community-based support groups, youths' friendship networks, parents and adolescent service providers, special youth-centered functions, and an advertised toll-free telephone line. Data collection occurred between July and October 1998.

A total of 184 self-identified gay, lesbian, and bisexual youths participated in the research (114 females and 70 males). Only female participants were included in the present study. Two women were unsure about their sexual orientation and were excluded from these analyses. The final study sample was comprised of 112 women, with 40% (n = 46) identifying as lesbians and 58% (n = 66) as bisexual. The sample was predominantly white (94%); mean age was 16.4 (SD = 1.2). Approximately 62% of the young women were recruited from youth groups, with 38% referred by friends or adolescent service providers. The majority lived with one or more parents (74%) and were still in high school (78%). Most lived in rural areas or small towns (60%) and the rest were from urban (27%) or suburban (13%) areas. Three-quarters (75%) perceived their families as middle class, 13% as low-income or poor, and 12% as working class.

Self-report questionnaires were administered directly by the Investigator. Written informed assent (under age 18) or consent (age 18) was obtained from all participants. Youths received $20 as a behavioral incentive for participating.

Measures

The measures discussed in this study comprised only a small part of the overall assessment. The three components included here were: (a) characteristics of dating relationships; (b) dating stress and violence; and (c) individual and social factors affecting relationships.

Characteristics of Dating Relationships. Recent dating history was assessed with questions that asked about the number, gender, and age of dating partners during the previous 12 months, the number of steady dating partners, length of relationships, and preferred dating activities. *Relationship satisfaction* was evaluated with a single item: "How satisfied are you with your relationship with your main partner?" (5-point scale; 0 = not at all, 4 = extremely). An open-ended question asked, "If there is anything you would like to be different about your relationship with your main partner, what would that be?" To assess *sexual activity,* youths were asked: "If you have been sexual with one or more persons in the past year (12 months), whom have you been sexual with? (This means sex that was your choice, that was *not* forced on you against your wishes.)" Response categories were: (0) I haven't been sexual with anyone, (1) men only, (2) women only, and (3) both men and women. To assess *lifetime sexual experiences,* two questions asked for the age at which participants' first consensual same-sex and opposite-sex sexual experiences occurred.

Dating Stress and Violence. To assess *stress* associated with "trying to find dating partners" and "breaking up with a girlfriend or boyfriend," participants were asked whether each event occurred in the last 6 months. If answered affirmatively, they were asked to indicate the effect it had on their lives using a 5-point Likert scale (1 = very bad effect; 5 = very good effect). *Suicidality* was measured using three items from the Youth Risk Behavior Survey (Centers for Disease Control, 1996) that ask about serious suicidal thoughts, making plans, and number of actual attempts during the past 12 months. *In-school victimization* was measured with nine items that asked youths the frequency with which they experienced specific forms of violence in their schools within the last 6 months because of their sexual orientation. Due to the low prevalence in the sample of the most serious violent acts, the items were aggregated into two categories of victimization (1 = experienced violence and 0 = did not experience violence) for each of the following measures: (a) Level I (verbal insults, threats of violence); and (b) Level II/Level III (objects thrown; personal property damaged; chased or followed; spit on; punched, kicked or beaten; sexually assaulted, or assaulted with a weapon) (Dean, Wu, & Martin, 1992; Hershberger & D'Augelli, 1995). *Dating violence* was assessed using six items. Participants were asked: "In any of your dating relationships during the past 12 months, have you or your partner: (a) thrown something that could hurt the other; (b) pushed or shoved the other in anger; (c) punched, hit, or slapped the other; (d) choked or kicked the other in anger; (e) forced the other to do something sexual that you or he/she did not want to do; and (f) verbally threatened to hurt the other." Items were coded 1 if the event occurred and 0 if it did not.

Individual and Social Factors. Participants rated their *openness with friends* and *openness with family* using 7-point Likert scales (0 = not open at all; 6 = totally open). *Self-esteem* was measured with the 10-item Rosenberg Self-Esteem Scale (Rosenberg, 1965). Statements were rated on a 4-point Likert scale ranging from *strongly agree* to *strongly disagree*. This measure has been used previously with sexual minority adolescents (D'Augelli & Hershberger, 1993; Savin-Williams, 1990). In this study, the Cronbach's alpha was .91.

RESULTS

Characteristics of Dating

Most of the women indicated having dated during the last 12 months, and typically dated more than one person. The majority was involved in same-sex dating, regardless of sexual orientation. Over one-third (38.5%) of the women dated only women, another 38.5% dated men and women, and 13% dated only men. The remaining 10% dated no one. Lesbians were significantly more likely than the bisexual women to date only women (74% versus 14%) and less likely to date only men (0% versus 23%) or both genders (22% versus 50%) ($\chi^2(3) = 44.13$, p $\leq$ .001).

Of the women who dated, 20% dated one person, nearly half (47%) dated two or three people, and 33% dated four or more, with no significant difference in number of dating partners based on sexual orientation. However, the lesbians averaged significantly more female dating partners (M = 2.7, SD = 2.0, range 1-12) than the bisexual women (M = 1.5, SD = 3.1, range 0-23), and fewer male partners (lesbians: M = .36, SD = .75, range 0-3; bisexuals: M = 2.5, SD = 3.0, range 0-16). The young women tended to date people around their own age; 56% dated individuals 2 years older or less; 17%, 3 or 4 years older; and 27%, 5 or more years older. On average, female partners were about 18.9 years old (range = 14 to 47 years); male partners were about 19 years old (range = 14 to 29 years).

Approximately half the women who dated had steady dating partners, including 52% of lesbians and 51% of bisexual women. Of these women, most (81%) had only one steady partner, with no significant difference between the lesbians and the bisexual women on the number of partners. The women engaged in a variety of typical adolescent dating activities with their steady partners, the most popular being going to the movies (60%), "hanging out" with each other or with friends (60%), and going out to eat (40%). Other activities mentioned were going for coffee; shopping; attending concerts or other cultural activities; and outdoor activities, such as hiking, swimming, and going to the beach.

Over one-third of the women (37%) reported involvement in a serious same-sex relationship, with lesbians significantly more likely to report such a relationship than the bisexual women (50% versus 26%; $\chi^2(1) = 6.00$, p $\leq$ .01). Most of these relationships were fairly new, with no significant difference in duration between the lesbians and bisexual women. One-quarter (25%) were involved for less than 1 month; 42% were involved between 1 and 6 months; 20% between 6 months and a year; and 14% for one year or longer. These percentages are nearly identical to those reported by D'Augelli and Hershberger (1993). Most of the women first met their primary partner in locales where heterosexual adolescents typically encounter their romantic partners, such as at school (24%), through friends (13%), or at special events and recreational settings, such as concerts, conferences, the beach, or coffeehouses (27%). Twenty-two percent met their partner at a sexual minority youth group meeting.

Overall, the young women felt quite satisfied with their primary relationship, with 67% indicating they were "very" or "extremely satisfied," and 25%, "a good amount" satisfied. The single most common problem cited was infrequent contact (35%), with seven women attributing this to geographical distance, and two indicating that parents prohibited them from seeing each other. One young women feared "That me and my girlfriend might break up because we don't see each other that much." Difficulties with honesty, trust and communication was the next most frequently mentioned problem (13%).

Consistent with previous research, the majority of the young sexual minority women (87%) reported having had lifetime consensual sexual experiences with both women and men partners, with no differences observed between lesbians and bisexual women. A small percentage of women (13%) reported never having a consensual sexual experience. Lesbians and bisexual women were equally likely to have had sexual experiences with men (59% and 73%, respectively). However, lesbians were significantly more likely than bisexual women to have had a sexual experience with another woman (89% versus 67%, respectively; $\chi^2(1) = 7.48$, p $\leq$ .01).

Most participants reported being sexually active during the past year (76%). The lesbians were more likely than the bisexual women to be sexually active with only women (78% versus 22%), and less likely to be sexually active with both genders (22% versus 45%) or with only men (0% versus 33%) ($\chi^2(3) = 28.62$, p $\leq$ .001). However, due to limitations of the data, the exact nature of the women's relationships with their sexual partners is unknown (e.g., friendship, dating, steady dating, primary relationship, or primarily sexual).

Dating-Related Stress

Trying to find a dating partner was evaluated as a negative event by only 22% of the lesbians and 15% of the bisexual women, although this difference was not significant. The majority of the young women had experienced a breakup within the previous 6 months (lesbians: 72%; bisexuals: 64%), with two-thirds indicating that these breakups exerted a negative impact on their lives. Although suicidal ideation was not significantly associated with experiencing a breakup, over one-quarter (26%) of the young women who reported suicidal ideation retrospectively attributed their suicidal thoughts to dating relationship problems. For the lesbians, however, making a suicidal plan was associated with experiencing a relationship breakup. Fisher's Exact Test revealed that a significantly greater proportion of the lesbians who made a suicidal plan experienced a relationship breakup (94%) than the lesbians who reported no suicidal plan in the last 12 months (60%), ($\chi^2(1) = 5.86$, p $\leq$ .02).

Interestingly, among the young women who were still in school (n = 94), dating status was found to be related to victimization within their schools for bisexual women. Significantly more bisexual women who were in steady dating relationships (74%) reported being the target of Level I victimization (e.g., verbal insults, threats of violence) than bisexual women without steady partners (42%) ($\chi^2(1) = 5.47$, p $\leq$ .05). Partner status did not increase the likelihood of in-school victimization for lesbians.

Verbal or physical abuse in dating relationships was reported to occur by over one-third of the women who had dated during the previous 12 months (N = 101). Bisexual women (44%) significantly more often reported some form of abuse than lesbians (25%), ($\chi^2(1) = 3.85$, p $\leq$ .05). Specifically, bisexual women were more likely to report being the target of threats of harm (26% vs. 9%, respectively; $\chi^2(1) = 4.76$, p $\leq$ .05) and choking (12% vs. 0%, respectively; ($\chi^2(1) = 5.76$, p $\leq$ .05). In addition, a minority of participants reported experiencing the following: pushing or shoving in anger (23%), throwing objects that could hurt (21%), punching, hitting, or slapping (13%), and forced sex (4%), with no differences based on sexual orientation. Due to limitations in the data collection, we do not know the nature of the participants' involvement in the abuse, the gender of the partners with whom these behaviors occurred (for the women who dated both genders), or whether the abuse transpired in recent past or current relationships. However, 28% of the women who had dated only women (N = 43) reported verbal or physical abuse in their dating relationships, indicating that such behavior was not restricted to the women's relationships with men.

Individual and Social Factors in Same-Sex Dating

Self-esteem was not significantly associated with involvement in same-sex dating or a primary relationship, or with relationship longevity or satisfaction. However, women who dated men had significantly lower self-esteem ($M = 30$) than the other women in the sample ($M = 32.4$, t = 2.25, p ≤ .05). Among the bisexual women, those with a steady partner had significantly lower self-esteem ($M = 27.7$) than those without a steady partner ($M = 32.1$, t = 2.97, p ≤ .01). Further, there was a significant negative association between bisexual women's self-esteem and the number of steady dating partners (r = −.35, p ≤ .01); their self-esteem decreased as their partners increased. No relationship between self-esteem and steady partner status existed for the lesbians.

The women involved in same-sex dating were significantly more open with their friends about their sexual orientation than were the other women ($M = 4.9$ versus 3.8, t = −2.57, p ≤ .01), as were the women involved in a primary same-sex relationship ($M = 5.2$ versus 4.3, t = −3.63, p ≤ .001). Openness with family members, however, was not significantly associated with same-sex dating or involvement in a primary relationship.

DISCUSSION

The results indicated that adolescent lesbians and bisexual women, despite many potential barriers, actively date, date several people over the course of a year, and enjoy primary same-sex relationships. Many of these young women meet their romantic partners in places frequented by adolescents and outside of organized gay and lesbian environments. They make themselves known to each other in schools, through friends and in recreational settings. Greater openness with peers about sexual orientation appears to facilitate same-sex dating, a finding consistent with research on the role of adolescents' peer networks in romantic relationships (Connolly & Johnson, 1996). Yet unknown is the role that heterosexual friends may play in introducing their gay, lesbian and bisexual friends to potential partners. Surprisingly, only 22% of these young women first met their primary partner at a sexual minority youth group. However, these groups play an important role in providing some adolescents with opportunities to meet and date similar-aged peers. As a source for dating partners, organized groups may be particularly important for young people who are less open about their sexual orientation in other youth-centered environments. Contrary to expectations, openness with family members about sexual orientation was not associated with same-sex dating or involvement in a primary relationship. Further research is needed to more fully understand the stress on, and the coping strategies used by, sexual minority youths who hide their relationships from their families.

This study's findings also point to risks associated with dating. The involvement of nearly 20% of the young lesbians in heterosexual sexual activity underscores the importance of counseling lesbians, as well as bisexual women, on both pregnancy prevention and HIV risk reduction. Relationship breakups may increase young women's suicidality, particularly for young lesbians who may have surmounted formidable obstacles to find and participate in an intimate relationship. These results also identify verbal and physical abuse as a reality in the relationships of these young women. Reported rates of adolescent dating violence range from 7% to 39% (Bennett & Fineran, 1998). Excluding the women who did not date, 25% of the lesbians and 44% of the bisexual women in this study experienced verbal or physical abuse in their dating relationships. Despite the limitations in the data, the results indicate that abusive behavior was not limited to male-female relationships, as 28% of the women involved in only same-sex dating reported some form of abuse.

The findings of this study suggest that adolescent bisexual women with steady partners are at heightened risk for verbal harassment if they are in school. Not only are they targeted for their sexual orientation, but their relationship choices may be ridiculed by peers and adults who equate bisexuality with simultaneous involvement with both genders. Consistent with research showing an association between going steady and low self-esteem in adolescent women (McDonald & McKinney, 1994), this study found that bisexual women with steady partners, but not lesbians, reported significantly lower self-esteem than their peers, as did women who dated men. McDonald and McKinney (1994) suggest two theoretical explanations that could apply to bisexual women: Steady dating, per Marcia (1993), constitutes a form of identity foreclosure, or, per Gilligan (1982), a way that young women lose their voices by limiting their choices. Low self-esteem could also be associated with the quality of their steady relationships, or with anxieties, fears and self-doubts over how to construct a life as a bisexual person in a world that polarizes sexuality. Programs and professionals serving adolescent lesbians and bisexual women should create opportunities for young people to discuss the myriad of problems and joys related to dating and romance, and assist them in developing problem-solving strategies and coping skills.

The findings of this study should be viewed with caution given several limitations. The methodological challenges in conducting research with sexual minority populations are well-documented (Sell & Petrulio, 1996). Like most research with this population, this study relied on a convenience sample of youths willing to disclose their identities. The sample was also predominantly white. The findings may not be generalizable to youths of color, self-identified youths who chose not to participate, and youths with same-sex attractions but not yet self-identified. The study was also limited to adolescents residing in northern New England who may differ in important ways (e.g., visibility and the resources available to them) from adolescents in other geographical regions. The cross-sectional nature of the data precludes statements of causality. Finally, youths were typically asked to report events and feelings experienced during the past 6 to 12 months, a method subject to recall bias and errors of memory (Bradburn, 1983).

In conclusion, this study demonstrated the resiliency of adolescent lesbian and bisexual women in constructing same-sex dating and romantic experiences, despite societal stigmatization and threats of victimization. Against all odds, these young women were actively creating a more normative adolescence for themselves, defying the culture's conspiracy of silence around same-sex dating, falling in love, and forming romantic relationships. The findings can guide youth-serving professionals in identifying youths' relationship concerns requiring supportive interventions.

REFERENCES

Bennett, L., & Fineran, S. (1998). Sexual and severe physical violence among high school students: Power beliefs, gender, and relationship. *American Journal of Orthopsychiatry, 68,* 645-652.

Bradburn, N.M. (1983). Response effects. In P.H. Rossi, J.D. Wright, & A.B. Anderson (Eds.), *Handbook of survey research* (pp. 289-328). New York: Academic Press.

Centers for Disease Control. (1996). Youth risk behavior surveillance-United States, 1995. *Morbidity and Mortality Weekly Report, 45*(No. SS-4).

Connolly, J.A., & Johnson, A.M. (1996) Adolescents' romantic relationships and the structure and quality of their close interpersonal ties. *Personal Relationships, 3,* 185-195.

D'Augelli, A.R., & Hershberger, S.L. (1993). Lesbian, gay, and bisexual youth in community settings: Personal challenges and mental health problems. *American Journal of Community Psychology, 21,* 421-448.

Dean, L., Wu, S., & Martin, J.L. (1992). Trends in violence and discrimination against gay men in New York City: 1984 to 1990. In G.M. Herek & K.T. Berrill (Eds.), *Hate crimes: Confronting violence against lesbians and gay men* (pp. 46-64). Newbury Park, CA: Sage.

Diamond, L.M. (2000). Sexual identity, attractions, and behavior among young sexual-minority women over a 2-year period. *Developmental Psychology, 36,* 1-10.

Diamond, L.M., Savin-Williams, R.C., & Dube, E.M. (1999). Sex, dating, passionate friendships, and romance: Intimate peer relations among lesbian, gay, and bisexual adolescents. In W. Furman, B.B. Brown, & C. Feiring (Eds.), *The development of romantic relationships in adolescence* (pp. 175-210). New York, NY: Cambridge University Press.

Elze, D.E. (1999). Risk and protective factors in mental health and behavioral functioning among sexual minority adolescents. *Dissertation Abstracts International*, 60(09), 3527. (University Microfilms No. 9945326).

Furman, W., Brown, B.B., & Feiring, C. (1999). (Eds.). *The development of romantic relationships in adolescence*. New York: Cambridge University Press.

Gilligan, C. (1982). *In a different voice: Psychological theory and women's development*. Cambridge, MA: Harvard University Press.

Herdt, G., & Boxer, A. (1993). *Children of Horizons: How gay and lesbian teens are leading a new way out of the closet*. Boston: Beacon Press.

Hershberger, S.L., & D'Augelli, A.R. (1995). The impact of victimization on the mental health and suicidality of lesbian, gay, and bisexual youths. *Developmental Psychology*, *31*, 65-74.

Hetrick, E., & Martin, A.D. (1987). Developmental issues and their resolution for gay and lesbian adolescents. *Journal of Homosexuality*, *14*(1/2), 25-43.

Marcia, J.E. (1993). The status of the statuses: Research review. In *Ego Identity: A Handbook for Psychosocial Research*. J.E. Marcia, A.S. Waterman, D.R. Matteson, S.C. Archer, & J.L. Orlofsky (Eds). New York: Springer-Verlag. pp. 22-41.

Martin, A.D., & Hetrick, E.S. (1988). The stigmatization of the gay and lesbian adolescent. *Journal of Homosexuality*, *15*, 163-183.

McDonald, D.L., & McKinney, P. (1994). Steady dating and self-esteem in high school students. *Journal of Adolescence*, *17*, 557-564.

Neeman, J., Hubbard, J., & Masten, A.S. (1995). The changing importance of romantic relationships to competence from late childhood to late adolescence. *Development and Psychopathology*, *7*, 727-750.

Pilkington, N.W., & D'Augelli, A.R. (1995). Victimization of lesbian, gay, and bisexual youth in community settings. *Journal of Community Psychology*, *23*, 34-56.

Sell, R.L., & Petrulio, C. (1996). Sampling homosexuals, bisexuals, gays, and lesbians for public health research: A review of the literature from 1990 to 1992. *Journal of Homosexuality*, *30*, 31-47.

Rosario, M., Hunter, J., & Gwadz, M. (1997). Exploration of substance use among lesbian, gay, and bisexual youths: Prevalence and correlates. *Journal of Adolescent Research*, *12*, 454-476.

Rosario, M., Meyer-Bahlburg, H.F.L., Hunter, J., Exner, T.M., Gwadz, M., & Keller, A.M. (1996). The psychosexual development of urban lesbian, gay, and bisexual youths. *The Journal of Sex Research*, *33*, 113-126.

Rosenberg, M. (1965). *Society and the adolescent self-image*. Princeton, NJ: Princeton University Press.

Rotheram-Borus, M.J., Hunter, J., & Rosario, M. (1994). Suicidal behavior and gay-related stress among gay and bisexual male adolescents. *Journal of Adolescent Research*, *9*(4), 498-508.

Rotheram-Borus, M.J., Rosario, M., Meyer-Bahlburg, H.F.L., Koopman, C., Dopkins, S.C., & Davies, M. (1994). Sexual and substance use acts of gay and bisexual male adolescents in New York City. *Journal of Sex Research*, *31*, 47-57.

Savin-Williams, R.C. (1990). *Gay and lesbian youth: Expressions of identity*. New York: Hemisphere Publishing.

Savin-Williams, R.C. (1996). Dating and romantic relationships among gay, lesbian, and bisexual youths. In R.C. Williams & K.M. Cohen (Eds.), *The lives of lesbians, gays, and bisexuals* (pp. 166-180). Fort Worth, TX: Harcourt Brace.

Savin-Williams, R.C., & Berndt, T.J. (1990). Friendships and peer relations. In S.S. Feldman & G.R. Elliott (Eds.), *At the threshold: The developing adolescent* (pp. 277-307). Cambridge, MA: Harvard University Press.

Sell, R.L., & Petrulio, C. (1996). Sampling homosexuals, bisexuals, gays, and lesbians for public health research: A review of the Literature from 1990 to 1992. *Journal of Homosexuality, 30*, 31-47.

The Impact of Group Membership on Lesbians' Physical Appearance

Ilana D. Krakauer
Suzanna M. Rose

SUMMARY. The impact of lesbian group membership upon physical appearance was examined among 81 young lesbians (ages 18-30) who participated in a questionnaire study. Most participants indicated making distinct but modest changes in their physical appearance after coming out as lesbians. These changes were in the direction of their pre-coming out conceptions of lesbians as being butch or androgynous in appearance. A majority reported cutting their hair shorter, wearing more comfortable shoes, or adopting a less traditionally feminine appearance after coming out. Participants also said they significantly less often wore dresses, used makeup, and shaved their legs and underarms. A significant decrease in body weight concern also occurred after coming out. Other changes in physical appearance are discussed. Participants believed that the changes were influenced by the opinions of other lesbians,

Ilana D. Krakauer, MA, is a doctoral student in the clinical psychology program at the University of Missouri-St. Louis. She serves as a student reviewer for *Psychology of Women Quarterly*. Her research is in the area of lesbian identity.

Suzanna M. Rose, PhD, is Director of the Women's Studies Center and Professor of Psychology at Florida International University. Her research focuses on romantic and friend relationships and lesbian and gay issues.

Address correspondence to: Ilana D. Krakauer, Department of Psychology, University of Missouri-St. Louis, St. Louis, MO 63121 (E-mail: idk141@studentmail.umsl.edu) or Suzanna M. Rose, Women's Studies Center, Florida International University, Miami, FL 33199 (E-mail: srose@fiu.edu).

[Haworth co-indexing entry note]: "The Impact of Group Membership on Lesbians' Physical Appearance." Krakauer, Ilana D., and Suzanna M. Rose. Co-published simultaneously in *Journal of Lesbian Studies* (Harrington Park Press, an imprint of The Haworth Press, Inc.) Vol. 6, No. 1, 2002, pp. 31-43; and: *Lesbian Love and Relationships* (ed: Suzanna M. Rose) Harrington Park Press, an imprint of The Haworth Press, Inc., 2002, pp. 31-43. Single or multiple copies of this article are available for a fee from The Haworth Document Delivery Service [1-800-HAWORTH, 9:00 a.m. - 5:00 p.m. (EST). E-mail address: getinfo@haworthpressinc.com].

31

their desire to signal prospective partners, and by becoming more comfortable with themselves. Implications of these results are discussed in terms of peer group norms, group identity, and sexual signaling. *[Article copies available for a fee from The Haworth Document Delivery Service: 1-800-HAWORTH. E-mail address: <getinfo@haworthpressinc.com> Website: <http://www.haworthPress.com> © 2002 by The Haworth Press, Inc. All rights reserved.]*

KEYWORDS. Lesbian, coming out, appearance, body image

Lesbian identity development has typically been conceptualized as the process of coming to know and accept one's sexual orientation as lesbian. Some changes that occur during the coming out process are intrapersonal, but many are interpersonal as well. If a newly out lesbian wants to become part of a lesbian community, she must find a way to demonstrate group membership. Physical appearance serves two important functions: it signals group membership and acts as a component of sexual signaling. Because these issues are likely to be salient for newly out lesbians, physical appearance is likely to change during the coming out period.

As a woman begins to present herself as lesbian, she must demonstrate that she belongs to the group. Physical alterations may carry great importance for a lesbian, and paying attention to one's dress is a way of signaling group membership (Cogan & Erickson, 1999; Rothblum, 1994). Especially at a time when one's family and heterosexual friends may be rejecting, approval from other lesbians is crucial. Therefore, newly out lesbians may turn to members of the lesbian community as experts. Many lesbians report taking cues from other lesbians when they first come out (Kitzinger & Wilkinson, 1995). We expected that the development of a lesbian identity would be reflected in changes in physical appearance, as women try to meet group standards or ideals. It is likely that such changes occur with greater strength when other lesbians suggest to a newly out lesbian that she does not "fit" in some way.

A second major function of physical appearance is to act as a sexual signaling system. One's attractiveness to and desire for women may be signaled by appearance. Because appearance has implications for dating, it becomes even more crucial to be recognized by and gain the approval of other lesbians. Studies of heterosexual dating have found that attractiveness plays a large role in who people like in both the short term and the long term (reviewed in Aronson, 1995). Attractiveness has been found to be central to sexual desirability among heterosexuals (Unger & Crawford, 1996). However, lesbians do not hold the same beauty standards as does the larger society (Blumstein & Schwartz, 1983). This discrepancy suggests that some aspects of a woman's physical appearance may change over time as she comes out as a lesbian. Standards concerning dress have varied historically among lesbian communities. For instance, the Daughters of Bilitis, a lesbian political organization that began in 1955, tried to counter the notion that lesbians were masculine, encouraging members to wear dresses and grow their hair long (D'Emilio, 1981). In other areas during the 1940s and 1950s, the standard for lesbians was either butch (stereotypically masculine) or femme (stereotypically feminine), and lesbians were supposed to commit to one or the other (Kennedy & Davis, 1993; Nestle, 1987). In the 1970s, middle class lesbians were expected to be feminists and to dress in an androgynous manner (Faderman, 1991; Newman, 1995). Currently, there seems to be a resurgence of interest in butch-femme (Munt, 1998), which has also been described as a "neo-femme renaissance," since the butch look has always been accepted to some extent among lesbians (Creith, 1996).

Lesbians may also have more room for variation in grooming than do heterosexual women. Wearing makeup, for instance, may be necessary in heterosexual contexts whereas it may be optional or even disapproved of in lesbian contexts. Body hair removal is another area where lesbians may have more room for personal variation. In a (presumably heterosexual) sample of college students, a woman with body hair was rated as less attractive than was the same woman without body hair (Basow & Braman, 1998). It has been suggested that the hairless ideal is sought in order to attract men (Basow & Braman, 1998). Lesbians may not seek to attain this ideal to the same extent as do heterosexual women. Lesbians may also be freer than heterosexual women to have a variety of hairstyles.

Other changes in lesbian appearance may have to do with nonverbal behavior, such as eye contact, posture, and stance. Because they are less overt than dress or speech, these behaviors may allow lesbians to recognize one another without risking societal disapproval. This may be particularly crucial when people do not feel that it is safe to publicly reveal their sexual orientation. By presenting herself in a manner that is subtle to the general public but recognizable to other lesbians, a lesbian may increase her chances of finding other lesbians in repressed or hostile environments. Among heterosexuals, men are rated as attractive when they maintain an open body posture and appear relaxed, but women with open body posture are rated as less attractive (Simpson, Gangestad, & Nations, 1996). It is interesting to speculate if this pattern would generalize to lesbians, who may reject the notion of women as submissive. Eye contact has also been cited as a way that lesbians recognize one another, and as a factor in lesbians' sexual approach one of another (Webbink, 1981).

The process of coming out as lesbian may also be accompanied by a shift in body weight concern. Because lesbians are socialized in the dominant society, it seems that they should be at equal risk for weight concern and eating disorders as are heterosexual women. However, lesbians seem to be under-represented in the eating-disordered population (Brown, 1987). It has been proposed that lesbian identity may act as a buffer that moderates the amount of negative attitudes about the female body and the extent to which a woman adheres to socio-cultural norms. For example, lesbians have reported higher ideal weight and more positive feelings for several aspects of their bodies than have heterosexual women (Bergeron & Senn, 1998). Likewise, heterosexual women in the same sample scored higher than did lesbians on a scale of internalization of societal norms. Research has also demonstrated that lesbians who were involved with lesbian/gay activities reported less concern about shape and less dieting behavior than did those lesbians not involved in community activities (Heffernan, 1996). Lesbians have rated weight as being the least important part of women's attractiveness, which suggests that lesbians may experience less pressure to conform to thin ideals (Heffernan, 1999). However, other studies have shown that lesbians do not significantly differ in body dissatisfaction from heterosexual women (Beren, Hayden, Wilfley, & Grilo, 1996). Additionally, lesbians have reported significant differences between their current and ideal weights (Cogan, 1999).

It seems likely that any buffering process is gradual, and that lesbians who have been out for longer will have less strongly negative feelings about their weight than will lesbians who have been out for less time. Thus, we hypothesized that women would report less body weight concern after coming out than they reported prior to coming out. We also expected that lesbians who had been out for a longer period of time would demonstrate less concern about their body weight than would lesbians who had more recently come out.

In summary, we examined the ways in which lesbian identity development affected physical appearance, including clothing, grooming, personal adornment (such as makeup and jewelry), nonverbal behavior, and body weight concern. It was expected that lesbians' physical appearance would become less stereotypically feminine along these dimensions from pre- to post-coming out.

METHOD

Participants

Lesbians between the ages of 18 and 30 (N = 81) were recruited from gay and lesbian community events and gathering places in a midwestern city to participate in the current research. The mean age of participants was 23 years (*SD* = 3.2). The majority (80%) was White and most had completed at least some college (81%). Two-thirds reported that they were in a committed relationship. Participants indicated that they first thought they might be lesbians at a mean age of 13 years (*SD* = 4.5) and were sure they were lesbians at a mean age of 18 years (*SD* = 3.1). Most reported being "very much" out to their heterosexual friends (*M* = 5.90, *SD* = 1.41) and their immediate families (*M* = 5.52, *SD* = 1.93) and moderately out at work (*M* = 4.46, *SD* = 2.35) (7-point scale, 7 = out to all). In addition, a majority (55%) reported at least some involvement with gay and lesbian community organizations.

Measures

Participants completed a paper and pencil questionnaire that included questions about physical appearance. These questions were part of a larger study. Participants were asked to describe several aspects of their physical appearance. Four open-ended questions asked about: (a) participants' pre-coming out conception of what "a lesbian" looked like, (b) changes they had made in their appearance after coming out, (c) the extent to which any changes in appearance were due to coming out, and (d) what they learned from other lesbians about what a lesbian "should" look like.

Additional quantitative measures asked participants to rate the following: how recognizable or visible they were as a lesbian in terms of appearance (6 items; 7-point scale, 7 = entirely); their reasons for making changes in their appearance after coming out (7 items; 7-point scale, 7 = very much); and their general reasons for dressing as they do (7 items; 7-point scale, 7 = very much). Participants also described how often they engaged in nine dress and grooming practices (e.g., wore makeup) at two points: (a) before coming out and (b) currently (9 items; 7-point scale, 7 = always). Participants were also asked to describe their favorite outfit.

Body weight concern was assessed with the Goldfarb Fear of Fat Scale (Goldfarb, Dykens, & Gerrard, 1985). This 10-item scale has high internal reliability (Cronbach alpha = .85), high test-retest reliability (r = .88), and demonstrates divergent validity between women with eating disorders, repeat dieters, and non-dieting women (Goldfarb et al., 1985). Items are rated on a 4-point scale (1 = very untrue, 4 = very true).

Finally, participants were asked to report their degree of involvement with the gay and lesbian community, their age at various stages of coming out, and the degree to which they were out to significant people in their lives. Demographic information also was requested.

Procedure

The first author reviewed the purpose of the study with the participants, who were invited to participate individually or in small groups.

RESULTS

As expected, lesbians reported making definite changes in their physical appearance after coming out. Taken as a whole, both the open-ended responses and ratings of physical appearance measures suggested that the changes were meant to convey group membership as well as to serve as a sexual signal to prospective lesbian partners. In response to the first open-ended question, participants' pre-coming out conceptions of what "a lesbian" looked like strongly resembled the classic butch lesbian stereotype. In response to this question, about 78% of participants (N = 63) described their pre-coming out notion of a lesbian as involving one or more of the following attributes or style of clothing: butch, masculine, short hair, stocky, muscular/athletic, no makeup, comfortable shoes, jeans, T-shirt, and/or leather jacket.

In their responses to the second open-ended question, most lesbians (73%) reported making changes in their appearance after coming out that were moderately in the direction of the butch stereotype. Four categories of appearance were described as being most affected, including getting a shorter haircut (57%), wearing more casual or masculine/androgynous clothes (43%), making changes in grooming habits such as no longer wearing makeup or shaving legs and underarms (20%), or getting a tattoo (36%) or body piercing (40%). Additionally, many participants reported a post-coming out weight gain (44%) or loss (39%), with 15% indicating that they had both gained and lost weight since coming out.

Third, coming out was viewed as most influential in the decision to get a body piercing (41%), followed by a change of hairstyle (38%), losing weight (32%), getting a tattoo (24%), and gaining weight (13%). The desires to convey group membership and signal prospective partners were among the reasons lesbians gave for changes in appearance. For example, one woman wrote: "women are attracted to more shorter haired lesbians," and another wrote, "I cut my hair to look more gay. I got another piercing in my ear because I thought it was the thing to do . . . I wanted to be recognized by other lesbians." Others were less sure of their reasons, like the participant who wrote that her haircut was "probably due to coming out. Needed outward physical change to match my inner change." Finally, some women felt that coming out gave them more freedom to be more fully themselves, such as a lesbian who wrote "I was no longer concerned [with] what boys found attractive so I was more comfortable dressing how I wished."

In a fourth open-ended question inquiring about "how other lesbians said you should look," a majority (63%) indicated they had been told to look more butch or androgynous if they wanted to be recognizable as a lesbian. Specific suggestions included getting a shorter haircut, wearing more T-shirts and tennis shoes or baggy, androgynous or masculine clothes, not shaving legs or underarms, cutting fingernails shorter, and acting more confident.

Ratings on the physical appearance measures paralleled the open-ended responses. As expected, participants indicated having made distinct changes in their appearance since coming out, on average, about five years ago. These changes tended to be moderate overall (see Table 1). On a 7-point scale (1 = not at all; 7 = entirely), participants' mean score for change of appearance was 3.61 (*SD* = 1.88) since coming out as lesbian. When asked the extent to which these changes were due to coming out, participants gave a mean rating of 3.39 (*SD* = 1.98), indicating the changes were somewhat attributable to the coming out experience. Most participants felt that they were somewhat recognizable as lesbians and rated various aspects of their appearance as slightly indicating to others that they were lesbian. Specifically, the item concerning "body language" was most highly endorsed, followed by eye contact, posture/stance, overall appearance, and clothing. As one participant wrote, "a straight person is very unlikely to [recognize me] because I am usually not that stereotypical. Another lesbian has a better chance of picking up on mannerisms, etc." However, some participants did not feel recognizable at all, like the woman who wrote "I don't think I look like what most people think lesbians look like."

Participants next rated the extent to which each of seven reasons had influenced the changes they had made in their appearance since coming out (see Table 1). "Grew more comfortable with myself" was the most highly rated item. As one participant wrote, "I felt more comfortable about myself. I realized who I was and that the best thing I could do would be to make myself happy with what I liked." "Other lesbians" was the next most highly endorsed reason. This was reflected in the response: "sometimes, I dress a little more masculine hoping other lesbians will recognize me as a lesbian and maybe conversation will ensue."

Participants also rated the importance of seven reasons for dressing as they do. Being comfortable and expressing their personalities received the highest ratings, followed by looking attractive and attracting women. One woman wrote, "there is a different aesthetic at work in the lesbian community than in the straight community. Therefore, though I'm still trying to appear attractive, the attempt has different manifestations (i.e., short hair, somewhat butchy clothes)."

TABLE 1. Mean Ratings for Items Assessing Lesbian Visibility and Reasons for Appearance (N = 81)

Measure	Mean	(SD)
Lesbian Visibility Items (7-point scale, 1 = not at all, 7 = entirely)		
How recognizable are you as a lesbian?	3.82	(1.93)
Identifiable as a lesbian by body language	4.36	(1.94)
Identifiable as lesbian by eye contact	4.26	(2.11)
Identifiable as lesbian by posture/stance	3.96	(2.05)
Identifiable as lesbian by overall appearance	3.89	(1.99)
Identifiable as lesbian by clothing	3.83	(1.92)
Reasons for Appearance Change (7-point scale, 1 = not at all, 7 = very much)		
Grew more comfortable with myself	5.73	(1.89)
Other lesbians	4.28	(2.14)
Age	3.91	(2.27)
Partner/lover	3.67	(2.27)
Feminist politics	3.49	(2.24)
Demands of job/work	2.87	(2.07)
Family	2.08	(1.47)
Reasons for Dressing as You Do (7-point scale, 1 = not at all, 7 = very much)		
To be comfortable	6.58	(0.99)
To express my personality	6.06	(1.29)
To look attractive	5.81	(1.30)
To attract women	4.86	(1.99)
To be accepted by other lesbians	2.98	(1.87)
To be accepted by heterosexuals	2.73	(1.83)
To make a political statement	2.39	(1.85)

Differences in the extent to which participants engaged in nine dress and grooming behaviors before coming out versus currently were assessed using t-tests. Significant differences in five behaviors were observed (see Table 2). In contrast to pre-coming out grooming practices, lesbians' current practices involved wearing comfortable shoes significantly more often and wearing makeup and dresses and shaving their legs and underarms significantly less often. No difference was found between pre-coming out and current frequency of wearing high heels, lingerie, earrings, or other jewelry. These changes might be related to peer group norms. For example, one participant wrote, "No

TABLE 2. Mean Ratings of Pre-Coming Out and Current Physical Appearance Measures[1]

Physical Appearance Items	Pre-coming out		Currently		
	Mean	SD	Mean	SD	t (80)
Wear comfortable shoes	5.96	(1.65)	6.31	(1.24)	−2.48*
Shave legs	6.09	(1.53)	6.15	(1.78)	2.43*
Shave underarms	6.59	(1.15)	6.15	(1.78)	2.20*
Wear makeup	3.23	(2.04)	2.66	(2.12)	2.08*
Wear dresses	2.90	(1.75)	2.50	(1.76)	2.01*
Wear high heels	2.27	(1.65)	2.04	(1.74)	1.40
Wear lingerie	2.52	(2.01)	2.56	(2.00)	< 1
Wear earrings	4.86	(2.38)	4.91	(2.53)	< 1
Wear other jewelry	5.25	(1.79)	5.56	(1.77)	−1.73

[1]Responses to the questions, "In non-work situations, please rate how often you did the following before coming out/currently." 7-point scale, 1 = not at all, 7 = always.
* $p < .05$

one told me how I should look, but as I got to know more about lesbians, I had more of an idea of what a lesbian might wear."

The last question focused on participants' favorite outfit. This question was aimed at providing a visual image of how young lesbians presented themselves. All but two participants wrote a specific description of their favorite outfit, and a majority of those responding (84%) described attire that was butch, masculine, or androgynous in appearance rather than traditionally feminine. Commonly mentioned items of clothing included the following:

- Pants (cargo pants, jeans, or comfortable shorts were mentioned frequently)
- Shirt (T-shirt, tank top, or button down shirt)
- Belt
- Jewelry (silver when mentioned)
- Comfortable shoes (Doc Martens, Birkenstocks, Tevas, sandals, boots, sports shoes)
- Colors (mostly black, blue, white, khaki, or camouflage)

A strong concern for appearance was reflected in the detail provided by some participants, particularly in terms of signaling group membership. For instance, one lesbian wrote: "My favorite outfit: a pair of button fly Levi baggy jeans, with this tan (khaki) color shirt with my blue and tan plaid shirt over it. I feel this outfit screams, 'I am a lesbian!'" Sexual signaling also was conveyed by clothing, as described by another participant who indicated her favorite outfit was: "[An] A-frame tank top (white), with big baggy khaki colored jeans with white stitching. Black belt. Black shoes. The ladies love it."

Finally, a one-way repeated measures ANOVA examined weight concern as measured by the Goldfarb Fear of Fat scale. Participants were classified into two Time Out groups (Out < 5 years; N = 41; Out ≥ 5 years; N = 40) using a median split based on time since coming out (defined as the age they felt sure they were lesbians). The repeated measures were the pre- and post-coming out scores of weight concern. As predicted, a significant interaction effect indicated that both coming out and length of time out had a significant effect on body weight concern, [F (1,79) = 4.93; $p < .05$). Lesbians had less body weight concern after coming out ($M = 17.07$, $SD = 5.93$) than before coming out ($M = 18.40$, $SD = 6.82$). In addition, lesbians who had been out longer than five years had less weight concern ($M = 15.70$, $SD = 4.55$) than lesbians who had been out less than five years ($M = 18.69$, $SD = 8.08$). Lesbians who were out longer than five years were also significantly older than lesbians who were out for less time ($M = 24.6$ vs. 21.8 years, respectively, $t(79) = -4.26, p < .005$).

DISCUSSION

As predicted, participants in the present study reported making clear changes in many areas of their physical appearance after coming out as lesbians in the direction of becoming more butch, masculine, or androgynous–or at least less feminine. These changes highlight the importance of peer group norms and support Blumstein and Schwartz's (1983) finding that lesbians have different beauty standards than does heterosexual society. The results of the present study are also consistent with Kitzinger and Wilkinson's (1995) sample, in which many participants reported taking cues from other lesbians when they first came out. The importance of peer group norms was evident in the responses of many participants. As one woman wrote, "Everyone likes my hair short better when compared to pictures they've seen of me with longer hair. One lesbian friend told me earrings 'didn't seem like me,' so I stopped wearing them. Everyone reinforces baggy clothes and big shoes and teases someone for dressing 'femmy.'"

Participants also reported a significant decrease in body weight concern after coming out. This is consistent with previous research suggesting that lesbians have less negative feelings about their bodies than do heterosexual women (e.g., Bergeron & Senn, 1998). Additionally, participants who had been out for longer reported less weight concern than did those who had been out for less time. This suggests that while lesbian ideals may be less thin or less extreme than heterosexual ideals, it takes time for a woman's body weight concern to decrease. This is consistent with the Beren, Hayden, Wilfley, and Streigel-Moore (1997) study that found similar body esteem between lesbian and heterosexual college students (assuming that most lesbian college students have been out for less time). However, several participants attributed their negative feelings about their bodies before coming out to adolescence. It could be that age is a factor in body weight concern as well as coming out, but it was not possible to separate the effect of age from length of time out in the present research.

There are several limitations to the current study. First, the generalizability of the results is limited. Because self-identified lesbians were recruited, the sample is unrepresentative in terms of degree of comfort with and disclosure of one's lesbian identity. Therefore, these results may not generalize to lesbians who do not publicly identify as such. The sample is also limited by age, because only lesbians between the ages of 18 and 30 were recruited. Therefore, the findings may be specific to this age group. Finally, the participants were mostly White, and were more highly educated than the general population. An additional limitation is that the retrospective design of the study may have had certain demand characteristics that could have influenced participants' responses.

In future research, it would be interesting to assess whether peer group norms are differentially important at different points of the coming out process. In this study, all participants were fairly young and many were in the early years of coming out. It is possible that as a woman's identity as a lesbian becomes more integrated into her identity as a person, peer group norms become less important. This possibility is reflected in the following participant's response: "I went through a period of all-out change . . . because I thought that's what I had to do to be a 'real' lesbian. Now, . . . I've basically gone back to being me–my hair is longer again, I wear my normal clothes. The changes for me were mental. I had to realize I was gay, and my appearance wasn't going to change that and make it any more true." Peer group norms may be less salient for lesbians who have been out for a longer time and who feel a greater sense of belonging to a lesbian community. This is consistent with Myers, Taub, Morris, and Rothblum (1999), who found that more newly out and younger lesbians and bisexual women experienced greater pressure about their appearance than did those women who were less newly out and were older. As lesbians age, they may not feel the same pressures to adopt a certain appearance as do younger lesbians. On the other hand, lesbians who have been out longer may feel even less influenced than younger lesbians by traditional feminine (heterosexual) beauty standards and may more strongly endorse the appearance norms of the lesbian community. Additionally, the need to signal other lesbians as sexual partners might remain relevant and encourage continued conformity to peer norms.

REFERENCES

Aronson, E. (1995). *The Social Animal*, Seventh Edition. New York: W.H. Freeman and Company.

Basow, S.A. & Bramen, A.C. (1998). Women and body hair: Social perceptions and attitudes. *Psychology of Women Quarterly, 22*, 637-645.

Beren, S.E., Hayden, H.A., Wilfley, D.E., & Grilo, C.M. (1996). The influence of sexual orientation on body dissatisfaction in adult men and women. *International Journal of Eating Disorders, 20*, 135-141.

Beren, S.E., Hayden, H.A., Wilfley, D.E., & Striegel-Moore, R.H. (1997). Body dissatisfaction among lesbian college students: The conflict of straddling mainstream and lesbian cultures. *Psychology of Women Quarterly, 21*, 431-445.

Bergeron, S.M. & Senn, C.Y. (1998). Body image and sociocultural norms: A comparison of heterosexual and lesbian women. *Psychology of Women Quarterly, 22*, 385-401.

Blumstein, P. & Schwartz, P. (1983). *American Couples*. New York: William Morrow and Company, Inc.

Brown, L.S. (1987). Lesbians, weight, and eating: New analyses and perspectives. In The Boston Lesbian Psychologies Collective (Ed.), *Lesbian Psychologies: Explorations & Challenges*, (pp. 294-309). Urbana, Illinois: University of Illinois Press.

Cogan, J.C. (1999). Lesbians walk the tightrope of beauty: Thin is in but femme is out. In J.C. Cogan & J.M. Erickson (Eds.), *Lesbians, Levis, and Lipstick: The Meaning of Beauty in our Lives* (pp. 77-89). Binghamton, NY: Harrington Park Press.

Cogan, J.C. & Erickson, J.M. (1999). Introduction. In J.C. Cogan & J.M. Erickson (Eds.), *Lesbians, Levis, and Lipstick: The Meaning of Beauty in our Lives* (pp. 1-9). Binghamton, NY: Harrington Park Press.

Creith, E. (1996). *Undressing Lesbian Sex: Popular Images, Private Acts, and Public Consequences*. London: Biddles Limited.

D'Emilio, D. (1981). Gay politics and community in San Francisco since World War II. In L.D. Garnets & D.C. Kimmel (Eds.) *Psychological Perspectives on Lesbian & Gay Male Experiences* (pp. 59-79). New York: Columbia University Press, 1993.

Faderman, L. (1991). *Odd Girls and Twilight Lovers: A History of Lesbian Life in Twentieth-Century America*. New York: Penguin Books.

Goldfarb, L.A., Dykens, E.M., & Gerrard, M. (1985). The Goldfarb Fear of Fat Scale. *Journal of Personality Assessment, 49*, 329-332.

Heffernan, K. (1996). Eating disorders and weight concerns among lesbians. *International Journal of Eating Disorders, 19*, 127-138.

Heffernan, K. (1999). Lesbians and the internalization of societal standards of weight and appearance. In J.C. Cogan & J.M. Erickson (Eds.), *Lesbians, Levis, and Lipstick: The Meaning of Beauty in our Lives* (pp. 121-128). Binghamton, NY: Harrington Park Press.

Kennedy, E.L. & Davis, M.D. (1993). *Boots of Leather, Slippers of Gold: The History of a Lesbian Community.* New York: Penguin Books.

Kitzinger, C. & Wilkinson, S. (1995). Transitions from heterosexuality to lesbianism: The discursive production of lesbian identities. *Developmental Psychology, 31,* 95-104.

Munt, S.R. (Ed.). (1998). *Butch/femme: Inside Lesbian Gender.* London: Cassell.

Myers, A., Taub, J., Morris, J.F., & Rothblum, E.D. (1999). Beauty mandates and the appearance obsession: Are lesbian and bisexual women better off? In J.C. Cogan & J.M. Erickson (Eds.), *Lesbians, Levis, and Lipstick: The Meaning of Beauty in our Lives* (pp. 15-26). Binghamton, NY: Harrington Park Press.

Nestle, J. (1987). Butch-femme relationships: Sexual courage in the 1950s. In J. Penelope & S. Wolfe (Eds.), *Lesbian Culture, An Anthology: The Lives, Work, Ideas, Art and Visions of Lesbians Past and Present* (pp. 107-112). Freedom, California: The Crossing Press, 1993.

Newman, L. (Ed.). (1995). *The Femme Mystique.* Boston: Alyson Publications, Inc.

Rothblum, E.D. (1994). Lesbians and physical appearance: Which model applies? In B. Greene & G.M. Herek (Eds.), *Psychological Perspectives on Lesbian and Gay Issues, 1,* 84-97.

Simpson, J.A., Gangestad, S.W., & Nations, C. (1996). Sociosexuality and relationship initiation: An ethological perspective of nonverbal behavior. In G.J.O. Fletcher & J. Fitness (Eds.), *Knowledge Structures in Close Relationships: A Social Psychological Approach* (pp. 121-146). Mahwah, NJ: Lawrence Erlbaum Associates, Inc.

Unger, R. & Crawford, M. (1996). *Women and Gender: A Feminist Psychology.* New York: The McGraw-Hill Companies, Inc.

Webbink, P. (1981). Nonverbal behavior and lesbian/gay orientation. In C. Mayo & N.M. Henley (Eds.), *Gender and Nonverbal Behavior* (pp. 253-259). New York: Springer-Verlag.

Butch/Femme in the Personal Advertisements of Lesbians

Christine A. Smith
Shannon Stillman

SUMMARY. Personal advertisements placed by lesbians were examined to determine how often butch/femme descriptors were used: (a) as a form of self-identification or (b) to indicate the type of partner being sought. The 388 personal advertisements were drawn from 16 alternative newspapers around the U.S., as well as from one Internet site (Qworld) that contained personal ads by lesbians. Each advertisement was coded for the presence or absence of butch/femme descriptors. The majority of advertisers did not mention butch or femme labels either in terms of self-identity or type of partner sought. Among the minority of advertisers who self-identified as butch or femme, more described themselves as femme than butch. Among advertisers seeking butch or femme partners, femme partners were sought most often. Explanations for the preference for femme lesbians were explored. *[Article copies available for a fee from The Haworth Document Delivery Service: 1-800-HAWORTH. E-mail address:*

Christine A. Smith is Assistant Professor of Psychology at Minnesota State University Moorhead. Previously, she taught at Lewis & Clark College and Ball State University. Trained as a Social Psychologist, her current research interests are collective self-esteem and gender self-presentation.

Shannon Stillman is a 2000 graduate of Lewis & Clark College. She is currently working with adolescent girls in the juvenile justice system. Her future plans are to attend graduate school in Social Psychology and Women's Studies.

Address correspondence to: Christine A. Smith, Department of Psychology, Minnesota State University Moorhead, Moorhead, MN 56563 (E-mail: casmith@mnstate.edu).

[Haworth co-indexing entry note]: "Butch/Femme in the Personal Advertisements of Lesbians." Smith, Christine A., and Shannon Stillman. Co-published simultaneously in *Journal of Lesbian Studies* (Harrington Park Press, an imprint of The Haworth Press, Inc.) Vol. 6, No. 1, 2002, pp. 45-51; and: *Lesbian Love and Relationships* (ed: Suzanna M. Rose) Harrington Park Press, an imprint of The Haworth Press, Inc., 2002, pp. 45-51. Single or multiple copies of this article are available for a fee from The Haworth Document Delivery Service [1-800-HAWORTH, 9:00 a.m. - 5:00 p.m. (EST). E-mail address: getinfo@haworthpressinc.com].

KEYWORDS. Lesbian, personal ads, dating, butch, femme

Butch and femme roles have been part of lesbian culture since the 19th century (Faderman, 1981). *Butch* is the lesbian slang term for women who feel more comfortable with masculine gender codes, styles, or identities than with feminine ones, whereas *femme* refers to lesbians who appear characteristically feminine (Rubin, 1992). The stereotypical lesbian couple consists of one butch and one femme. Butch and femme have been described as complementing one another in an erotic system in which the butch was expected to be both the doer and the giver; the butch was fulfilled by the femme's passionate response to her (e.g., Kennedy & Davis, 1993). The desire for a femme partner has been described as one of the fundamental components of butch identity (Ennis & Lloyd, 1995). At least one survey of lesbian identity confirmed the idea that butch lesbians tend to prefer femme partners. Loulan (1990) reported that about 50% of butch lesbians indicated a preference for femme partners, whereas 25% preferred butch partners and 25% indicated no preference. No research has been done of preferences of self-identified femmes.

Although butch/femme roles have been enduring, the degree to which they have been accepted within the lesbian community has varied greatly. Butch/femme style was prevalent among poor and working-class lesbians, but by the 1950s, the roles began to be rejected by middle-class lesbians who favored adopting "a mode of behavior and dress acceptable to society" (Daughters of Bilitis Newsletter, 1957-67, cited by Faderman, 1991, p. 180). In the 1970s, during the second wave of the feminist movement, the roles continued to remain in disfavor, particularly among middle-class lesbians who favored an androgynous appearance. Butch and femme roles were reported to have resurfaced in the 1980s and 1990s primarily among young, urban, middle- and upper-class lesbians (e.g., Ennis & Lloyd, 1995; Stein, 1992). However, new combinations of butch/butch and femme/femme couples were increasingly visible (Faderman, 1981; Ennis & Lloyd, 1995).

In the current study, we sought to determine what proportion of lesbians identified themselves as butch or femme when looking for partners through personal ads and the extent to which butch/femme partners or pairings were sought. Personal ads that include same-sex listings tend to be found in alternative newspapers and Internet sites that cater to urban, middle-class patrons. Thus, individuals placing personal ads are not representative of the lesbian community as a whole. However, personal ads are one publicly available base of information about lesbian partner selection practices.

We expected to find that the majority of lesbians would not self-identify as either butch or femme based on the trends described above and on the limited amount of research available. For instance, Weber (1996) interviewed a diverse sample of lesbians and found that 26% identified themselves as butch, 34% as femme, and 40% as "independent." Butch and femme were defined primarily by physical appearance. Additionally, social class was a significant determinant of butch/femme identity. Lesbians with more education and with higher incomes were less likely to identify as butch or femme. Similarly, Bailey, Kim, Hills, and Linsenmeier (1997) reported in their study of personal ads that a majority identified themselves as feminine and indicated a preference for feminine partners. Thus, we predicted that the majority of individuals who placed personal ads would not include butch or femme as descriptors. However, when descriptors were specified, self-identification as femme and a preference for femme partners were expected to occur more often than were butch self-identification and partner preference.

METHOD

Personal ads were taken from "alternative" newspapers from around the United States as well as one Internet site (Qworld). Sixteen newspapers were selected to represent each region of the United States. Papers and ads were obtained through travel, requests, and from their Websites. At least two editions of each newspaper were included in order to get a larger, more representative sample of each newspaper. A total of 388 advertisements by lesbians were examined from the "women seeking women" section of the paper or site. All ads for women seeking women within a paper were selected. Advertisers who were specifically seeking only sexual partners were excluded from the sample, as were advertisers who identified as bisexual. The racial breakdown of advertisers was as follows: No race specified (56%); Black (22%); White (18%); Hispanic (3%); and Asian American (1%).

Each ad was coded for the presence or absence of butch/femme descriptors in terms of (a) self-identification and (b) type of partner sought. Terms such as "soft butch," "stone butch," and "masculine" were coded as butch labels; femme labels included "ultra fem," "high femme," or "lipstick lesbian." Approximately 50% of advertisements were coded by the two authors to 90% agreement. Each author then coded half of the subsequent advertisements.

RESULTS

As predicted, significantly more lesbians (75%) who placed personal ads did not self-identify as butch or femme, compared to the percentage of those who did self-identify as either femme (14%) or butch (11%), (χ^2(2, N = 388) = 303.78, p ≤ .01). Likewise, in terms of type of partner sought, most ads (66%, N = 256) did not specify butch/femme descriptors. The following were typical ads:

Looking for fun. I'm 28yo, honest, respectful and considerate. Would love to find a similar woman to go out to dinner with, movies and long walks on the beach. Must be an animal lover.

Complex girl seeks same. Girl, 22, into indie rock, writing & pop culture, seeks quirky, sexy, emotional girl to love & comfort me. I'm a fat curly-haired feminist. UB charming & open minded.

GBF, professional, intelligent, attractive, seeking GF 39-49. Interests: sports, travel, museum & music. Friendship & possible LTR.

Also as expected, significantly more advertisers specified no butch/femme labels when seeking other lesbians (66%) than preferred butch or femme, but when labels were specified, significantly more ads used femme descriptors (26%) than butch (5%) (χ^2(2, N = 388) = 246.53, p ≤ .01). In fact, twelve ads (3%) explicitly indicated a "no butches" request.

Self-identified femme advertisers (N = 55) were significantly more likely to request other femmes as partners (56%) than butches (18%), with some expressing no butch/femme preference (25%) (χ^2(2) = 13.56, p ≤ .01). In addition, thirty-seven advertisers who did not identify as butch or femme specifically requested femme partners.

Gay white female wants you if you are feminine, free, caring, kind, and loving. Let's get together for fun and laughs and ?? No drinkers/drugs.

Feminine seeking feminine professional, GBF, mid 30s, 125 lbs., looking for another woman for friendship, and possibly more. Please no butches or heavy women. I enjoy movies, travel, reading, eating out, and cultural events.

SGWF seeks SBi/GF, feminine, 28-35, for friendship and more. Must like children. Light smoker. Drug/disease free. Must be honest, serious, and responsible.

The 42 self-identified butch lesbians tended significantly more often to request femme partners (74%) than butch partners (7%) or partners with no descriptors (19%) ($\chi^2(2) = 31.86, p \leq .01$). Additionally, eight advertisers who did not specify any descriptors for themselves sought butch partners. The following ads are typical of those advertisers identifying as butch or seeking butch partners.

> Attractive GF, soft butch, black hair/eyes. Educated, down-to-earth, financially stable, sensitive, loving and caring. Seeking GW/HF, 25-40, who's professional, very feminine, and bright to do things with: dinner, movies, etc.

> Serious and sincere SGWF, 45, down-to-earth, romantic, soft butch, not big on bars but likes to dance, smoker but hope to quit. Looking for age 30-49. Weight proportionate, personality and chemistry a plus.

> Wanted butch. GWF, 5'3", 135, Dark hair/hazel eyes, romantic. Seeking GW/Latina F 36-40 something butch who enjoys dinners/walks on the beach/movies & quiet nights.

> GWF, 30, soft butch, seeks GWF, 32-40, butch, into art, movies, dancing and having a good time. No smokers, Bis, or men.

In sum, the results indicate that feminine partners were the most sought after, regardless of how the advertiser identified herself (if she did identify as butch or femme). However, most advertisers neither identified themselves as butch or femme nor requested butch or femme partners.

DISCUSSION

The suggestion that butch/femme roles are enjoying a resurgence of popularity was not supported by the results of our research on lesbians' personal advertisements. The majority of personal ads we examined did not include butch or femme descriptors for either the purpose of (a) self-identification or (b) partner preference. In fact, butch/femme roles appeared to be relatively absent or unpopular among lesbians as assessed by the content of personal ads. This may be the result of the visibility of butches as opposed to femmes. Since butch women are more likely to be perceived as lesbian, those who are seeking butches may have an easier time finding them. Individuals seeking femmes may be more likely to use personal ads because the relative invisibility of femmes (is she a femme or a straight woman?) makes it more difficult to identify femmes. Thus, those seeking femmes may rely on personal ads to find femmes that might otherwise be invisible. If this is the case, butch women are not necessarily less desirable, but easier to find without a personal ad.

Self-identification as femme was more common among the minority of advertisers who used butch/femme labels to describe themselves. Similarly, the minority of advertisers who had butch/femme partner preferences was more likely to seek femme partners. These results have two main implications. First, they support previous research by Weber (1996) and Bailey et al. (1997), indicating that lesbians desire feminine qualities in partners. Ennis (1998) suggested that if one scans personal ads, one will find more ads for lesbians requesting butch partners than femme partners. Our findings directly contradict this and suggest that butch partners are not highly desirable. Second, the results suggest that lesbians do not necessarily adhere to the stereotypical butch/femme pairing. The finding is consistent with Faderman (1981) and Ennis (1998), who concluded that there is little evidence that lesbians conform to the stereotype of the butch/femme couple. One exception in our results was the finding that self-identified butch women did tend to request femme partners. Thus, a small percentage of lesbians did appear to conform to the stereotype.

There are several possible explanations for our findings. First, the lack of butch/femme descriptors in this study may reflect a class bias. Most of the ads came from alternative, independent papers from major cities. Readers tend to be young, educated, and middle-class. If butch/femme has primarily been associated with working-class lesbians, then our findings may underestimate the desirability of butch/femme pairings among that group. Second, the preference for femme self-identification and partner preference, when such designations occurred, suggested that lesbians may endorse the social norm of femininity as being more desirable for women. However, further research would need to be undertaken to determine if lesbians' definitions of "femme" correspond to cultural standards of "femininity." A third possible explanation for advertisers being more likely to identify as femme is that femme lesbians might have more difficulty in finding dates than butch lesbians because they are less visible and may be mistaken as heterosexual. However, in the medium of the personal ad, femme lesbians can indicate that they are indeed lesbians.

In conclusion, the findings suggest that butch/femme roles may not be enjoying a renewed popularity among lesbians, as other writers have suggested. The findings do indicate, however, that butch and femme roles have not disappeared and are desirable for a segment of lesbians. Future research might examine specific content of butch and femme personal ads. For example, are self-identified butches or femmes more likely to offer physical descriptors or specific personality characteristics? Do individuals seeking butch partners also request masculine personality characteristics or suggest stereotypically masculine activities? A number of writers have argued that butch and femme are more than imitations of masculine and feminine roles associated with traditional heterosexual coupling (Rubin, 1992; Ennis, 1998). Future research on personal ads may examine whether advertisers seem to associate femme and butch with other activities traditionally associated with stereotypical masculine or feminine behavior.

REFERENCES

Bailey, J.M., Kim, P.Y., Hills, A., & Linsenmeier, J.A. (1997). Butch, femme, or straight acting? Partner preferences of gay men and lesbians. *Journal of Personality and Social Psychology, 73*, 960-973.

Ennis, S. A. (1998). Flunking basic gender training. In D. Atkins (Ed.) *Looking queer: Body image and identity in lesbian, bisexual, gay, and transgender communities.* New York: Harrington Park Press.

Ennis, S. A. & Lloyd, M. (1995). "G. I. Joes in Barbie land": Recontextualizing butch in twentieth-century lesbian culture. *National Women's Studies Association Journal, 7*, 1-23.

Faderman, L. (1981). *Surpassing the love of men.* New York: William and Company.

Faderman, L. (1991). *Odd girls and twilight lovers: A history of lesbian life in twentieth-century America.* New York: Columbia University Press.

Kennedy, E. L. & Davis, M. (1993). *Boots of leather, slippers of gold: The history of a lesbian community.* New York: Routledge.

Loulan, J. (1990). *The lesbian erotic dance: Butch, femme, androgyny and other rhythms.* San Francisco: Spinsters.

Rubin, G. (1992). Of catamites and kings: Reflections on butch, gender, and boundaries. In J. Nestle (Ed.), *The persistent desire: A femme-butch reader* (pp. 466-482). Boston: Alyson Publications, Inc.

Stein, A. (1992). All dressed up, but no place to go? Style wars and the new lesbianism. In J. Nestle (Ed.), *The persistent desire* (pp. 431-439). Boston: Alyson.

Weber, J.C. (1996). Social class as a correlate of gender identity among lesbian women. *Sex Roles, 35*, 271-279.

Lesbians in Love:
Why Some Relationships Endure
and Others End

Kristin P. Beals
Emily A. Impett
Letitia Anne Peplau

Kristin P. Beals is a graduate student of Social Psychology at the University of California, Los Angeles. She has begun a line of research to examine the association between stigma management and well-being. Her first paper discusses how decisions regarding disclosure affected the romantic relationships of gay men and lesbians. Her current studies are focusing on possible processes that may explain the association between disclosure of a minority sexual orientation and psychological and physical well-being.

Emily A. Impett is a student in the doctoral program in Social Psychology at the University of California, Los Angeles. Her research focuses on how people's feelings of acceptance by intimate partners influence how they feel about themselves and how they maintain important intimate relationships. Applying this general interest to the sexual domain, one line of research examines how people's relative commitment to a partner and perceived power in a relationship influence their willingness to consent to unwanted sexual activity and their ability to successfully negotiate safe sexual interactions with a partner.

Letitia Anne Peplau is Professor of Social Psychology at the University of California, Los Angeles. She has published many empirical papers on gender and close relationships, including studies of lesbian, gay male, and heterosexual relationships. In 2000, she co-edited (with Linda Garnets) a volume of the *Journal of Social Issues* on "Women's Sexualities: New Perspectives on Sexual Orientation and Gender." She was the 1997 recipient of the Distinguished Scientific Achievement Award from the Society for the Scientific Study of Sexuality.

Address correspondence to: Kristin P. Beals, UCLA Department of Psychology, Graduate Mail Room, Los Angeles, CA 90095-1563 (E-mail: kbeals@ucla.edu).

[Haworth co-indexing entry note]: "Lesbians in Love: Why Some Relationships Endure and Others End." Beals, Kristin P., Emily A. Impett, and Letitia Anne Peplau. Co-published simultaneously in *Journal of Lesbian Studies* (Harrington Park Press, an imprint of The Haworth Press, Inc.) Vol. 6, No. 1, 2002, pp. 53-63; and: *Lesbian Love and Relationships* (ed: Suzanna M. Rose) Harrington Park Press, an imprint of The Haworth Press, Inc., 2002, pp. 53-63. Single or multiple copies of this article are available for a fee from The Haworth Document Delivery Service [1-800-HAWORTH, 9:00 a.m. - 5:00 p.m. (EST). E-mail address: getinfo@haworthpressinc.com].

SUMMARY. Lesbians often begin romantic relationships with high hopes that their relationships will be satisfying and long-lasting. Why do some women maintain committed and stable relationships while others do not? This article considers factors that affect commitment and stability among lesbian couples. We begin by reviewing previous empirical research on the topic. Next, we test a leading model of commitment using survey data from 301 lesbian couples who participated in the American Couples Study (Blumstein & Schwartz, 1983). According to Caryl Rusbult's model (1983), an individual's commitment to a relationship is affected by three general factors: satisfaction, the quality of alternatives to the current relationship, and investments made in the relationship. In turn, a woman's degree of commitment influences relationship stability. Path analysis provided strong support for Rusbult's model. Nonetheless, this model did not fully explain the sources of commitment and stability in lesbian relationships. Consequently, we consider unique aspects of the social environment that may affect commitment and stability in lesbian relationships. *[Article copies available for a fee from The Haworth Document Delivery Service: 1-800-HAWORTH. E-mail address: <getinfo@haworthpressinc. com> Website: <http://www.HaworthPress.com> © 2002 by The Haworth Press, Inc. All rights reserved.]*

KEYWORDS. Lesbians, couples, relationships, relationship satisfaction, commitment, stability, minority stress

Successful love relationships are a core ingredient for personal happiness and psychological well-being (Myers, 1993). Yet intimate relationships begun with high hopes sometimes end in painful disappointment. Why do some lesbians maintain committed and long-lasting intimate relationships while others do not? Relationship researchers have identified three general factors that affect relationship commitment and stability.

A first factor concerns positive attraction forces that make partners want to stay together. In general, a relationship is satisfying when it provides many rewards, such as a partner's great sense of humor, enjoyment of joint activities, or feeling loved. A relationship is also satisfying if it entails relatively few costs, such as conflict or a partner's annoying habits (Duffy & Rusbult, 1986; Kurdek, 1994). Research shows that lesbians in a couple relationship typically report very positive feelings for their partners and rate their current relationship as highly satisfying and close (see review by Peplau & Spalding, 2000). Researchers have begun to identify factors that enhance or detract from satisfaction in lesbian relationships. Lesbian couples tend to be happier when the partners are similar in attitudes and values (Kurdek & Schmitt, 1987), and perceive their relationship as fair and equal in power or decision making (Eldridge & Gilbert, 1990; Kurdek, 1998; Kurdek & Schmitt, 1986; Peplau, Padesky, & Hamilton, 1982; Schreurs & Buunk, 1996). Individual characteristics including values about relationships (Eldridge & Gilbert, 1990; Peplau, Cochran, Rook, & Padesky, 1978) and neuroticism can also make a difference (Kurdek, 1997).

A second factor affecting the longevity of a relationship is the availability of alternatives. These could include another potential romantic partner, but also having more time to devote to friends or work or, for some people, enjoyment of time alone. Research has found that lesbians who perceive more available alternatives are less committed (Duffy & Rusbult, 1986; Kurdek & Schmitt, 1986). In contrast, the lack of desirable alternatives can be an obstacle to ending a lesbian relationship. This finding helps to explain why some women remain in relatively unhappy partnerships.

Finally, commitment is also affected by barriers that make it difficult for a person to leave a relationship (Kurdek, 1998). Barriers include anything that increases the psychological, emotional, or financial costs of ending a relationship. Examples would include pooling financial resources, sharing a loved pet, developing a network of mutual friends, or time already spent in the relationship. Of particular importance are those investments of time, money, or other resources that would be lost if a relationship ended. In a longitudinal study of lesbian relationships, Kurdek (1998) found that barriers to leaving the relationship were a significant predictor of relationship stability over a 5-year period.

In a useful analysis of relationship commitment, Caryl Rusbult (1983) has integrated these three factors. According to her model, an individual's personal commitment to maintain a relationship is strong when the relationship is highly satisfying, when alternatives are few or unattractive, and when partners have invested many resources in the relationship. Commitment influences whether couples stay together or break up. The goal of the current study was to test Rusbult's model of relationship commitment in a large sample of lesbians who were living with a romantic partner. A further goal was to test whether lesbians' initial level of commitment to their relationships predicted which couples stayed together and which terminated their relationships over an 18-month period.

METHOD

The current study entailed secondary analyses of data collected by sociologists Philip Blumstein and Pepper Schwartz (1983) as part of the American

Couples Study (ACS). Participants were recruited nationwide in 1978 and 1979 through television, radio, newspapers, and magazines. Volunteers were mailed two copies of a questionnaire, one for each partner, although the current study analyzed data from only one partner. Eighteen months after the women completed the initial questionnaire, a follow-up questionnaire was mailed to a randomly chosen subsample (59%) of lesbian couples. Seventy-five percent of these lesbian couples completed the follow-up. To be included in the original ACS sample lesbian couples had to live together at least four days a week, have had a sexual relationship at some point, and "consider themselves a couple not just roommates" (Blumstein & Schwartz, 1983, p. 7). Only those women who completed the 18-month follow-up were included in the current analyses. For further details of recruitment and data collection, see Blumstein and Schwartz (1983).

Participants

The 301 lesbian women in cohabiting relationships came from all regions of the country, with greatest representation from the Middle Atlantic, North Central U.S., California, and Hawaii. Most participants (95%) were White. Participants varied considerably in age, education, and religion. The modal participant was a 32-year-old with a college degree who worked full-time. The modal couple had been together for 2-3 years, although relationship length varied from less than a year to 33 years.

Measures

Participants were instructed to complete the questionnaires separately and not to discuss their responses until they had returned the surveys. The 40-page questionnaire contained questions about each woman, her partner, and aspects of their relationship. The questionnaire contained items that were conceptually similar to measures of commitment, satisfaction, investments and quality of alternatives used by Rusbult (Rusbult, Martz, & Agnew, 1998). In constructing measures of these variables, we followed Rusbult's general strategy of creating indexes with multiple items whenever possible.

Satisfaction. Participants rated how satisfied they were with their relationship in general on a 9-point scale (1 = *extremely satisfied* to 9 = *not at all satisfied*). They also indicated their satisfaction with four more specific aspects of their relationship: "how we express our affection," "my amount of influence in decision making," "our social life" and "our sex life." Scores were reversed so that higher scores indicated greater satisfaction. The reliability coefficient for the 5 items was high (alpha = .82).

Quality of alternatives. Participants were asked, "If something were to happen to your partner and you were forced to live without her, how difficult would it be for you to find another partner?" and "If something were to happen to your partner and you were forced to live without her, how difficult would it be for you to avoid loneliness?" on 9-point scales (1 = *extremely difficult* to 9 = *not at all difficult*). The reliability coefficient for these two items was alpha = .47.

Investments. Two items assessed the investment of money: "Do you and your partner have a joint checking account?" and "Do you and your partner have a joint savings account?" (1 = *yes* and 2 = *no*). Two items assessed time already spent in the relationship: the number of years the partners had dated and the number of years they had lived together. A final question asked, "What proportion of your close friends are also your partner's friends?" (1 = *all*, 5 = *half*, 9 = *none*). Scores were reversed so that high scores represented more investments in the relationship; the alpha was .71.

Commitment. A single item captured each woman's commitment to her relationship. Participants answered the question, "How likely is it that you and your partner will still be together five years from now?" on a 9-point scale (1 = *extremely likely* to 9 = *not at all likely*). Scores were reversed so that high scores represented more commitment to the relationship.

Relationship stability. Assessment of relationship stability was based on a question included in the follow-up questionnaire mailed 18 months after completion of the first questionnaire. Participants were asked if they were still living with their partner (*full-time, part-time,* or *not*). Responses to this question were recoded to create a dichotomous measure of stability (1 = *do not live together* and 2 = *live together either full-time or part-time*).

Strategy for Data Analysis

We used path analysis in the EQS computer program (Bentler, 1995) to test the hypothesized associations among variables, as well as the overall fit of the model.[1]

RESULTS AND DISCUSSION

The lesbian women in this sample were very satisfied with their relationships; the mean satisfaction score was 7.5 on a 9-point scale (*SD* = 1.04). The women also reported low levels of alternatives; their mean scale score of 2.8 on a 9-point scale (*SD* = 1.90) indicated that the women thought they would have considerable difficulty finding a new partner or avoiding loneliness if the relationship ended. Further, women indicated relatively high levels of investment. Forty percent of partners had a joint checking account and 47% had a joint savings account. In addition, 88% of the women reported that more than half of their friends were also friends of their partner and 24% of women indicated that all of their friends were also friends with their partner. Finally, most women were strongly committed to maintaining their relationship at the time of the first questionnaire; the mean commitment score was 7.8 on a 9-point scale ($SD = 1.77$). In short, consistent with prior research (Peplau & Spalding, 2000), most lesbian women in this sample reported being in happy, committed relationships. Further, during the 18-month follow-up period, only 12% of the lesbian couples broke up. Would Rusbult's model help us to understand which couples remained together and which did not?

Testing Rusbult's Model of Commitment and Stability

The primary goal of this study was to test the adequacy of Rusbult's model in a sample of cohabiting lesbian women. Results of the path analysis are shown in Figure 1. As anticipated, the model fit the data quite well, and all indices of the adequacy of the fit were in acceptable ranges, χ^2 (3, N = 301) = 5.13, $p = .16$, CFI = .98, RCFI = .98, RMSEA = .06.

In addition to testing the fit of the model, we also tested theory-based predictions about factors that increase commitment in women's relationships. As ex-

FIGURE 1. Testing the fit of Rusbult's model using path analysis.

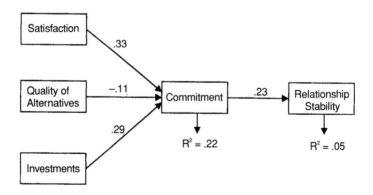

Note: The independent variables (i.e., satisfaction, alternatives and investments) were allowed to freely covary; for ease of reading, however, the correlations are not shown in this figure. All path coefficients represented were significantly different from zero ($p < .05$). Standardized path coefficients are presented.

pected, we found that satisfaction, quality of alternatives, and investments each were statistically significant and unique predictors of lesbians' commitment to a relationship. As depicted in Figure 1, all paths were significant, although satisfaction was a much stronger predictor of commitment than either alternatives or investments. As in previous research with heterosexuals, we found that a lesbian's commitment to a partner depended not only on satisfaction, but also on the quality of alternatives and the extent to which the woman had already invested in her relationship. In combination, these three variables predicted 22% of the variance in commitment. We also tested the hypothesized causal link between commitment at initial testing and whether or not the couple stayed together 18 months later. As shown in Figure 1, lesbians' initial commitment significantly predicted relationship outcomes, accounting for 5% of the variance in stability.

Taken together, these results provide solid support for the value of Rusbult's model in understanding factors that influence both commitment and stability in lesbian relationships. In addition, these findings extend the generalizability of the theoretical model by demonstrating its applicability to same-sex relationships. There are commonalties in the ingredients that contribute to committed and enduring love relationships regardless of partners' sexual orientation.

Understanding Commitment and Permanence in Lesbian Relationships

It is also clear that factors other than those identified by Rusbult affect lesbian couples. In our analyses, Rusbult's model accounted for only 22% of the variance in commitment and 5% of the variance in stability. In contrast, an earlier study using path analysis to test Rusbult's model among heterosexual couples, satisfaction, investments and alternatives predicted 48% of the variance of commitment and commitment accounted for 20% of the variance in stability (Bui, Peplau, & Hill, 1996). Both methodological and conceptual factors may have limited our ability to predict commitment and stability in lesbian relationships. As in all secondary data analysis, we relied on measures constructed for other purposes that may not have adequately assessed our key variables. Stronger results might be found using more detailed measures. Further, relatively few of the lesbian couples (12%) broke up during the 18-month follow-up time period. This is not surprising since couples had been together for an average of 3.7 years at initial testing. In contrast, the Bui et al. study of heterosexuals began within the first year of dating, and followed participants for 15 years. Stronger results for lesbians might have been found had we initially surveyed women just forming relationships and followed them for a longer time period.

Conceptual limitations to Rusbult's model may be equally important. In particular, Rusbult's model does not consider the environmental context within which lesbian intimate relationships exist. In America today, prejudice against sexual minorities represents a unique aspect of the social environment that can color many aspects of lesbian (and gay male) relationships. It is understandable that a model developed initially to understand heterosexual relationships might not give prominence to contextual influences. Most heterosexual couples navigate in a social environment that typically ranges from benign to positively supportive. In contrast, efforts to understand same-sex relationships may require an explicit examination of the social context. Three examples illustrate how this approach might be useful.

A stressful environment caused by unemployment, illness or other life problems can take its toll on any couple. Because of their sexual orientation, lesbians and gay men are at risk for additional types of stress, sometimes called "minority stress." For example, lesbians are vulnerable to major stressful life events, including hate crimes and discrimination (DiPlacido, 1998; Gillows & Davis, 1987). In addition, lesbians may also experience minor but persistent stress from such daily hassles as having to conceal their sexual identity or hearing insulting jokes or comments about homosexuality. Research investigating the impact on lesbian relationships of these and other types of minority stress would be valuable, and might enhance our understanding of forces that can undermine the longevity of same-sex partnerships.

A second example concerns the management of a stigmatized lesbian identity. Because of widespread prejudice toward sexual minorities, lesbians must carefully manage when and how to reveal versus conceal their sexual orientation to others. One study found that issues about disclosure were a source of conflict in some lesbian couples (Murphy, 1989). We know very little about how lesbian couples negotiate the management of their individual and couple identity or about the impact of these decisions on relationship quality.

A third contextual factor concerns the social and legal institution of marriage. For heterosexuals, marriage provides special rights and privileges for partners that can strengthen relationships. Marriage also erects barriers to the ending of relationships, such as the costs of divorce, investments in joint property, concerns about children, or a wife's financial dependence on her husband. Further, marriage is a symbol of a couple's commitment and pledge to stay together "for better or for worse." As a result, marriage may strengthen commitment and stability. Currently lesbian couples cannot marry legally, are less likely than heterosexuals to have children or property in common, and are usually dual-earner couples. Lesbians experience neither the special benefits of marriage nor the obstacles to dissolution that marriage often entails. As a result, lesbians may be less likely to become trapped in a hopelessly miserable and deteriorating relationship, but may also be more inclined to end a relationship that might have improved if given more time and effort. In recent years, lesbians and gay men have initiated activities to provide some of the privileges and protections of heterosexual marriage, for instance, through policies extending domestic partnership benefits to same-sex couples, by the use of formal commitment ceremonies, and by efforts to legalize same-sex marriage. Information about the impact of these changes on lesbian relationships is lacking.

Finally, research on the social context of lesbian relationships should consider not only the effects of sexual prejudice and discrimination, but also the impact of efforts by lesbians and gay men to create their own supportive social environments. Lesbian and gay communities and institutions can offer support and validation for same-sex couples. Some lesbians create extended networks of friends or a "family of choice" to provide the sense of acceptance that may not always be available from their family of origin. Research about the creative ways in which lesbians construct positive and supportive social environments for themselves and their relationships would be valuable.

ACKNOWLEDGMENTS

This research used the *American Couples*, 1975-1978, data set [made accessible in 1992, computer data]. These data were collected by Philip Blumstein and Pepper Schwartz and are available through the archive of the Henry A. Murray Research Center of Radcliffe College, Cambridge, Massachusetts (Producer and Distributor). This study was funded by a grant to Letitia A. Peplau from the UCLA Academic Senate Committee on Research, and is based on work supported under a National Science Foundation Graduate Fellowship awarded to Emily A. Impett.

NOTE

1. Parameter estimates were based on maximum likelihood estimation using a covariance matrix. Four indices of model fit were used. The chi-square statistic tests whether the hypothesized model adequately explains the observed pattern of data. A non-significant chi-square indicates good model fit, although it is directly related to sample size. In contrast, the Comparative Fit Index (CFI), the Robust Comparative Fit Index (RCFI) and the Root Mean Square Error of Approximation (RMSEA) are computed independent of sample size. The CFI ranges from 0 to 1.0, with values greater than .90 considered acceptable (Bentler, 1990). Because many of the variables were skewed, we will also report the Robust Comparative Fit Index (RCFI), an alternative estimation method commonly used when multivariate normality does not hold. Finally, the RMSEA index measures the amount of residual between the observed and predicted covariance structure and compensates for the effect of model complexity (Steiger & Lind, 1980). RMSEA values less than .08 are considered acceptable (Browne & Cudeck, 1993). For comparable analyses testing Rusbult's model among married couples from the American Couples Study, see Impett, Beals, & Peplau (2001-02).

REFERENCES

Bentler, P. M. (1990). Comparative fit indexes in structural models. *Psychological Bulletin, 107*, 238-246.

Bentler, P. M. (1995). *EQS structural equations program manual.* Encino, CA: Multivariate Software, Inc.

Blumstein, P., & Schwartz, P. (1983). *American couples: Money, work, sex.* New York: Morrow.

Browne, M. W., & Cudeck, R. (1993). Alternative ways of assessing model fit. In K. A. Bollen & J. S. Long (Eds.), *Testing structural equation models* (pp. 136-162). Newbury Park, CA: Sage.

Bui, K. T., Peplau, L. A., & Hill, C. T. (1996). Testing the Rusbult model of relationship commitment and stability in a 15-year study of heterosexual couples. *Personality and Social Psychology Bulletin, 22*(12), 1-23.

DiPlacido, J. (1998). Minority stress among lesbians, gay men, and bisexuals: A consequence of heterosexism, homophobia, and stigmatization. In G. M. Herek (Ed.), *Stigma and sexual orientation: Understanding prejudice against lesbians, gay men, and bisexuals* (pp. 138-158). Thousand Oaks, CA: Sage.

Duffy, S. M., & Rusbult, C. E. (1986). Satisfaction and commitment in homosexual and heterosexual relationships. *Journal of Homosexuality, 12*(2), 1-24.

Eldridge, N. S., & Gilbert, L. A. (1990). Correlates of relationship satisfaction in lesbian couples. *Psychology of Women Quarterly, 14*, 43-62.

Gillow, K. E., & Davis, L. L. (1987). Lesbian stress and coping methods. *Journal of Psychosocial Nursing, 25*(9), 28-32.

Impett, E. A., Beals, K. P., & Peplau, L. A. (2001-02). Testing the investment model of relationship commitment and stability in a longitudinal study of married couples. *Current Psychology, 20*(4), 312-326.

Kurdek, L. A. (1998). Relationship outcomes and their predictors: Longitudinal evidence from heterosexual married, gay cohabiting, and lesbian cohabiting couples. *Journal of Marriage and the Family, 60*(3), 553-568.

Kurdek, L. A. (1997). Relation between neuroticism and dimensions of relationship commitment: Evidence from gay, lesbian, and heterosexual couples. *Journal of Family Psychology, 11*, 109-124.

Kurdek, L. A. (1994). The nature and correlates of relationship quality in gay, lesbian, and heterosexual cohabiting couples. In B. Greene & G. M. Herek (Eds). *Lesbian and gay psychology: Vol 1* (pp.113-155). Thousand Oaks, CA: Sage.

Kurdek, L. A., & Schmitt, J. P. (1987). Partner homogamy in married, heterosexual cohabiting, gay, and lesbian couples. *Journal of Sex Research, 23*, 212-232.

Kurdek, L. A., & Schmitt, J. P. (1986). Relationship quality of partners in heterosexual married, heterosexual cohabiting, and gay and lesbian relationships. *Journal of Personality and Social Psychology, 51*, 711-720.

Murphy, B. C. (1989). Lesbian couples and their parents: The effects of perceived parental attitudes on the couple. *Journal of Counseling and Development, 68*, 46-51.

Myers, D. G. (1993). *The pursuit of happiness.* New York: Avon.

Peplau, L. A., Cochran, S. D., Rook, K., & Padesky, C. (1978). Women in love: Attachment and autonomy in lesbian relationships. *Journal of Social Issues, 34*(3), 7-27.

Peplau, L. A., Padesky, C., & Hamilton, M. (1982). Satisfaction in lesbian relationships. *Journal of Homosexuality, 8*(2), 23-35.

Peplau, L. A., & Spalding, L. R. (2000). The close relationships of lesbians, gay men and bisexuals. In C. Hendrick & S. S. Hendrick (Eds.), *Close relationships: A sourcebook* (pp. 111-124). Thousand Oaks, CA: Sage.

Rusbult, C. E. (1983). A longitudinal test of the investment model: The development (and deterioration) of satisfaction and commitment in heterosexual involvements. *Journal of Personality and Social Psychology, 45*, 101-117.

Rusbult, C. E., Martz, J. M., & Agnew, C. R. (1998). The investment model scale: Measuring commitment level, satisfaction level, quality of alternatives, and investment size. *Personal Relationships, 5* (4), 357-391.

Schreurs, K. M. G., & Buunk, B. P. (1996). Closeness, autonomy, equity and relationship satisfaction in lesbian couples. *Psychology of Women Quarterly, 20*, 577-592.

Steiger, J. H., & Lind, J. C. (1980, May). *Statistically based tests for the number of common factors.* Paper presented at the annual meeting of the Psychometric Society, Iowa City, IA.

Not Any One Thing:
The Complex Legacy of Social Class
on African American Lesbian Relationships

Ruth L. Hall
Beverly Greene

SUMMARY. The complex legacy of social class on African American lesbians in relationships was examined using a case study approach. Six highly educated, middle class African American lesbians in their mid-thirties to mid-fifties were interviewed in this exploratory study. Differences in social class were perceived as the reason for the conflict in these relationships. Conversely, similarities in social class were described as making relationships operate more smoothly. Although similarities in race can generate shared cultural values, it is the meaning given to a couple's perceived similarities and differences that influences the quality of the communication between partners. These preliminary

Ruth L. Hall, PhD, is Associate Professor in the Department of Psychology at The College of New Jersey and a licensed psychologist. She received her PhD in clinical psychology from Boston University in 1979 and her MEd in sport psychology from Temple University in 1996.

Beverly Greene, phD, ABPP, is Professor of Psychology at St. John's University and a certified clinical psychologist in private practice. A Fellow of the American Psychological Association and the Academy of Clinical Psychology, she is a Diplomate of the American Board of Professional Psychology in Clinical Psychology.

Address correspondence to: Ruth Hall, PhD, Department of Psychology, The College of New Jersey, P.O. 7718 Ewing, NJ 08628-0718 (E-mail: ruthhall@tcnj.edu), or Beverly Greene, PhD, Professional Psychology Program, St. John's University, Jamaica, NY 11439 (E-mail: Bgreene203@aol.com).

[Haworth co-indexing entry note]: "Not Any One Thing: The Complex Legacy of Social Class on African American Lesbian Relationships." Hall, Ruth L., and Beverly Greene. Co-published simultaneously in *Journal of Lesbian Studies* (Harrington Park Press, an imprint of The Haworth Press, Inc.) Vol. 6, No. 1, 2002, pp. 65-74; and: *Lesbian Love and Relationships* (ed: Suzanna M. Rose) Harrington Park Press, an imprint of The Haworth Press, Inc., 2002, pp. 65-74. Single or multiple copies of this article are available for a fee from The Haworth Document Delivery Service [1-800-HAWORTH, 9:00 a.m. - 5:00 p.m. (EST). E-mail address: getinfo@haworthpressinc.com].

findings highlight a previously unexplored contribution to the dynamics in African American lesbian relationships. *[Article copies available for a fee from The Haworth Document Delivery Service: 1-800-HAWORTH. E-mail address: <getinfo@ haworthpressinc.com> Website: <http://www.haworthPress.com> © 2002 by The Haworth Press, Inc. All rights reserved.]*

KEYWORDS. African American, lesbian, race, social class, racism

Creating safe environments in which to live, work, and love is essential to the mental and physical health of African American lesbians. Our triple minority status–woman, African American and lesbian–adds daily challenges to our ability to do so. Most research on African American lesbians has focused on how we cope with these multiple oppressions (e.g., see Hall & Greene, 1996 for a review). However, in addition to prejudice and discrimination, African American lesbians also must deal with relationship issues that have not been the focus of research. One area that we have identified in our clinical work as creating friction within African American lesbian relationships was difference in social class backgrounds. Class is a recurrent theme raised by clients, usually indirectly, and is a frequent topic in discussions with friends and colleagues. Using a case study approach, we will present an exploratory analysis showing how a small sample of African American lesbians reported being affected by discrepancies in social class within their relationships.

THE COMPLEX LEGACY OF SOCIAL CLASS

An African American lesbian is not any one thing. Each woman is a complexity of multiple identities that include both her internal world as well as the sociopolitical matrix of her life (Greene, 2000). According to Hill-Collins (1998), "the distinctive yet interlocking structures of oppression" (p. 233) that an African American woman experiences cannot be fully appreciated using a Western linear analysis. The oppressions are not simply additive; rather, they all function simultaneously and with differing degrees of intensity. In fact, one aspect of identity may take precedence at different times and in different situations. For instance, an African American lesbian may be discriminated against in one situation due to her race, but be privileged in another by virtue of her education or social class. Partners may assume that race is enough without taking into account that their interpretation of similarities can transform them into what can become compelling differences.

Having to continually cope with being different might well be a distinguishing feature of African American lesbian identity. Not only are African Americans visibly different from the dominant cultural group in the United States, but being a lesbian may exacerbate a sense of being different within their African American community. As a result, an African American lesbian may experience herself as so unlike her family and unlike the broader society that she may be reticent to set herself apart any further by creating more difference, particularly from her family. For example, she may feel that having a partner from another social class or race may further separate her from her family and her choice might be experienced as a threat to her family value system. Similarly, problems may ensue for a couple if one woman's lesbianism is more openly accepted by her family than her partner's is.

Being in a romantic relationship adds yet another level of complexity to the experience of similarity and difference. The meaning of one's race and sexual orientation are likely to be different for each person in a couple, even in same-race relationships. Although difference sometimes is viewed as an asset in relationships, difference can be a source of conflict that can become irreconcilable (Mays, 1985). Our clinical experience attests to the fact that partners often perceive their differences to be the locus of challenges and problems in their relationships, when problems exist. When those problems are not present and partners perceive themselves as similar, they attribute the absence of those problems to their similarities. We feel that the personal meaning of similarities and differences affects the degree that either will be seen as a challenge within domestic relationships among African American lesbians.

We also contend that the meaning assigned to differences and similarities by individuals is influenced to a great degree by the dynamics in the family of origin and the meaning assigned to difference and sameness within that family. When difference in one's family of origin has been treated as if it were a flaw in a person, differences in other relationships may trigger the sense that one is "wrong" or that the partner is "wrong" in some way. Similarly, if similarities between family members are devalued or result in an individual feeling unseen or unheard, difference may have a positive value. In our clinical work, we have observed that the inability to experience differences from one's partner as positive or potentially positive, and the tendency to view similarities as if they have no problematic aspects, is a common problem among African American lesbians seeking therapy. The degree to which difference was encouraged, accepted, or tolerated, or discouraged, denied, or punished in each woman's family of origin often plays a significant role in these conflicts. The family legacy of how differences were treated influences an African American lesbian's view of herself and her partner.

Some differences may be perceived as more threatening than others, particularly when they are characteristics that are associated with dominant cultural values, identities, status or prestige. We have observed a pattern in which one woman, seeing herself as defective or lacking, tries to improve her status by selecting a partner who possesses characteristics valued by the dominant culture, i.e., who is educated or of a higher class standing. The partner who sees her lack of education or middle class standing as a defect may fear being abandoned by her more educated partner if "someone better comes along" and attribute her devalued view of herself to her partner. That sense of inferiority and insecurity about the relationship contributes to the partner with the dominant cultural identity being experienced as a threat, reflected in accusations that she has "lost her roots" or "acts superior."

In contrast to the problems associated with differences, many African American lesbians say that sharing an ethnicity with a partner created a substantive common bond. Mays, Cochran, and Rhue (1993) discussed the importance of a shared cultural context in understanding the intimate relationships of African American women. Similarities in race, gender, sexual orientation, and social class can create a foundation of similar life experiences, including a shared cultural context and similar experiences with oppression. However, shared physical similarities often lead to the assumption of shared life experiences and values that may not be present. Because the experience of the same race, gender, sexual orientation, and social class may be very different among group members, similarities along these dimensions may also lead to assumptions of sameness and a resulting harmony in relationships that is unwarranted. When this happens, partners may be disappointed when these expectations are not met and feel betrayed by their partner. While it is commonly assumed that relationships in which partners are similar along these important dimensions might be easier to negotiate, determining what actually constitutes a similarity beyond shared group membership is more difficult to assess.

In the case studies presented below, we explored the impact of differences on African American lesbians' relationships. The case studies were based on open-ended interviews conducted by the first author with six well-educated, primarily middle-aged African American lesbians, ages 35 to 55. Two of the participants were a couple. This retrospective analysis by a non-representative sample was not meant to be descriptive of African American lesbians as a whole. Rather, it was intended as a starting point that might be useful in illuminating some previously unstudied aspects of African American lesbians' relationships. Our case studies are similar to the issues many of our lesbian clients bring into therapy. Each participant had been involved with at least one partner whom they described as being markedly different in terms of social class and at least one partner whom they described as being similar on this dimension.

Participants were invited to talk freely about how the differences and similarities had influenced those relationships. Each participant indicated that differences in social class were a source of discord in their relationships. All stated that being in a relationship with a partner who was similar in class was easier. The case studies reflect participants' views that difference is more difficult to manage in a relationship and that similarities in terms of social class make class a non-issue. However, we do not suggest that these preliminary findings adequately represent the problems or outcomes associated with differences in relationships. Nor do we believe that difference in class necessarily means that a relationship will fail. Differences must be acknowledged and recognized as a source for potential problems in communication just as similarities, though less obvious, may be problematic as well. The perception that differences are disruptive forces and that similarities create harmony leads to problems in relationships.

We also experience that African American families, independent of class, share common bonds that interact with class differences. For example, African Americans tend to maintain closer relationships with their family of origin than white lesbians (Greene, 2000). For African Americans, family of origin usually includes biological relatives as well as fictive kin (non-blood related individuals who become part of the family). The normative African American family may be less likely to reject a lesbian outright (Greene, 2000). However, African American families are likely to institute a silent "don't ask, don't tell" policy, where acknowledgment of sexual orientation or recognition of one's partner remains unstated. African American lesbians' relationships are perceived to inherently create less dissonance than interracial lesbian relationships even when class is an issue. There is a presumed buffer of similar cultural values that is presumed to be absent in mixed race relationships. We contend, however, that these presumptions are often incorrect and may be problematic for a variety of reasons. Our participants also stated that maintaining a relationship with a partner who differed from them in class involved more work but that there were advantages to such relationships.

Social Class

Social class is an elusive concept as applied to African Americans. Typical definitions of social class still take into account income, education and occupation (Hollingshead & Redlich, 1958). Wyche (1996) suggested that when applied to African Americans, social class must take into account values in the African American community that concern prestige and status. In the African American community the application of middle class values rather than the attainment of middle class fiscal status create the African American middle class. Thus, African Americans from blue collar families–usually dual income families–effectively function as the middle class in many communities; however, unlike their white counterparts, they do so because they rely on two incomes. Furthermore, a defining feature of middle class values among African Americans is an emphasis on education.

Social class standing also affects a family's discretionary income. For example, many African American families heavily supplement extended family members' household expenses and frequently are involved in raising a relative's child. The meaning of discrepancies between partners in social class background may lead to conflicts about both the value of education and financial decisions. The case studies below illustrate the experiences of six African American lesbians in their relationships and the influence of social class backgrounds.

Case Study 1: Jennifer and Sylvia

Jennifer, a 35-year-old African American lesbian in a professional level job, described how differences in social class backgrounds affected her current relationship with Sylvia, a 40-year-old African American blue-collar worker. Jennifer's family, with its middle class values, strongly encouraged her to get a college education. In contrast, Sylvia received no encouragement from her family to attend college. In fact, Sylvia's family perceived getting an advanced degree and adopting a middle class lifestyle as "putting on airs." Thus, Sylvia was threatened by Jennifer's educational achievement and feared losing her to a more educated woman. Sylvia owns the home that she and Jennifer live in rather than having joint ownership. This was a direct result of her concern with being abandoned by Jennifer. They discussed this issue when it arose, but it remained a chronic source of argument. Conflicts over money also seemed to originate in the couple's social class differences. Jennifer liked vacation travel and felt entitled to treat herself to such. Sylvia was reluctant to travel because of the expense, but also because of the paucity of people of color in many vacation areas. Jennifer and Sylvia entered couples' counseling to come to terms with these differences. That Jennifer and Sylvia can openly discuss their differences has strengthened their relationship and provided them with a solid foundation for coping with ensuing differences.

Case Study 2: Callie and Nancy

Callie, a 47-year-old African American lesbian professional, chose to reflect on the eight-year relationship she had with Nancy that ended some years ago. Callie has a graduate degree and grew up in a dual income family that had middle class values. Nancy, an African American lesbian about the same age as Callie, grew up in a low income family. As an adult, Nancy worked in factory and pink-collar jobs. Nancy was adamant about maintaining working class values in order to stay close to her family. Nancy's family was negative about getting an education and Nancy had denied herself opportunities to attend college. Yet Nancy always selected middle class women with advanced degrees, like Callie, as partners. It was as if Nancy was living by proxy in her relationships. However, Nancy consistently reminded her partners of their class difference and criticized their middle class values. Although class difference was not a significant issue early in their relationship, class and education emerged as stumbling blocks when Callie began working in an educational setting. This environment became a source conflict and was one factor that led to the end of their relationship.

Case Study 3: Dianne and Helen

Dianne, a 53-year-old African American lesbian professional, described herself as being from a working class Black family that had middle class values. Dianne's former partner, Helen, was from a wealthy, white family and was also a professional. Differences in values about spending plagued the relationship. Helen liked to go on costly vacations and out for expensive dinners, but Dianne was reticent to do so. She assumed that these activities were amenities of the upper class. When traveling, Dianne liked to stay with relatives and friends whenever possible in order to visit at length; Helen wanted to stay in a hotel regardless of the cost to have more privacy. Dianne and Helen also had different values about social etiquette. Helen frequently criticized Dianne for not demonstrating appropriate manners and codes of conduct. For example, if Dianne talked "too loud" or engaged in an animated discussion while out to dinner, Helen got upset. Dianne, in turn, disliked the sense of entitlement Helen seemed to have regarding service industry people. Any time Dianne tried to discuss class differences with Helen an argument ensued, leaving both feeling unsupported and misunderstood by each other. According to Dianne, these conflicts helped her realize that their marked class and family value differences, although recognized, may have been a chronic source of disagreement. Even though they continued in their relationship, the cumulative effect of "non-topics" that included differences in class and family values led to its demise.

Case Study 4: Kim and Nicole; Kim and Denise

Kim, a 48-year-old African American lesbian professional, felt that class differences were a major factor in the breakup of her previous long-term relationship. Kim was raised in an urban low-income neighborhood. Kim felt that her former partner, Nicole (also a professional), who was raised in a middle class African American family, was paternalistic toward Kim and her family due to class differences. Nicole was quick to point out differences in their values and to assess Kim and her family negatively. Their class difference also meant a difference in access to resources. Kim's family did not have the resources to help her obtain a college education. Kim was fortunate to find a mentor who gave her the confidence and encouragement to seek out college and a professional career. Kim did not find these issues to be present in her current relationship with Denise (also a professional) because both she and Denise came from struggling families, could appreciate each other's educational achievements, and "fit in" with each other's families.

Case Study 5: Stephanie and Carla

Stephanie, age 48, and Carla, age 42–both professionals–were an African American lesbian couple who had been together for four years and who spoke about how the similarity of their social class background led to similarities in values. Both women were from a solidly dual income, middle class family and hailed from the same metropolitan area. Their families' values about education and financial success were similar. Stephanie indicated that they both had to deal with the internalized racism they learned from the Black middle class (e.g., "don't act too Black"), as well as issues around skin color and hair texture. Both women stated that a difference in class background had been a source of conflict in prior relationships, but that their similarities on this dimension eliminated it as a stressor in their relationship with each other.

* * *

In sum, the five case studies presented here illustrate the importance of recognizing class differences in relationships. It is imperative that any couple take time to explore how class enters into their personal value system and how class is then transmitted into a relationship. It is presumed that similarities in class eliminate it as a primary source of conflict. We want to emphasize, however, that it is the meaning assigned to specific class backgrounds that determines whether or not class difference will be problematic. Differences can be bridged as long as the dialogue remains open and each partner is willing to examine and potentially modify her behavior.

CONCLUSION

Our exploratory investigation of how social class background affects African American lesbian relationships suggests that class difference is perceived a major source of conflict in some relationships. Each of the women we interviewed experienced significant problems in at least one important relationship that they attributed to class. Furthermore, all of the participants attributed the breakup of at least one relationship specifically to conflicts about class differences. Clearly there are additional components that enhance or compromise a relationship, and class similarities and differences are just one aspect of a relationship. Since class is closely tied with family expectations, values, and experiences, we suggest that any analysis of working or compromised relationships examine the partners' understanding of their class backgrounds as intervening factors. Scholars who study relationships must become aware of the complexity of class as a phenomenon and of how class differences/similarities affect relationships. Broader understandings of this phenomena may be helpful to couples attempting to engage in healthy relationships.

AUTHOR NOTES

Dr. Hall is a member of the Women's Sports Foundation Advisory Board. Her research addresses people of color, women, and athletes. She was a recipient of the Association for Women in Psychology's (AWP) Women of Color Psychologies Award for her publication "Mind and Body: Toward the Holistic Treatment of African American Women" (Hall, 1998). She is also an associate editor of the *Encyclopedia of Women and Sport in America* (1998). In 1995, Dr. Hall received AWP's Christine Ladd-Franklin Award for outstanding service to AWP and to feminist psychology. Dr. Hall recently served as the President of Section One (Black Women) of APA's Division 35 and a Fellow of the American Psychological Association. She also maintains a private practice and consults with various agencies and organizations.

An editorial board member of numerous scholarly journals, Dr. Greene has served as founding co-editor of Psychological Perspectives on Lesbian, Gay and Bisexual Issues (Sage), a series of annual publications sponsored by Division 44 of APA. Dr. Greene is the sole editor of the series' third volume, *Ethnic and cultural diversity among lesbians and gay men,* and co-editor of the recently published fifth volume: *Education, Research and Practice in Lesbian, Gay, Bisexual and Transgendered Psychology: A Resource Manual.* Dr. Greene is a recipient of numerous national awards for distinguished professional contributions and publications, including the APA Division 35's 2000 Heritage Award; 1995, 1996 and 2000 Psychotherapy with Women Research Awards (Div. 35); and 1991, 1995, and 2000 Women of Color Psychologies Publication Awards (AWP). She is co-editor of the recently published *Psychotherapy with African American Women: Innovations in Psychodynamic Perspectives and Practice* (Guilford Press).

REFERENCES

Greene, B. (2000). African American lesbian and bisexual women in feminist psychodynamic psychotherapy: Surviving and thriving between a rock and a hard place. In L.C. Jackson & B. Greene (Eds.), *Psychotherapy with African American women: Innovations in psychodynamic perspectives and practice* (pp. 82-125). New York: Guilford Press.

Hall, R. L. & Greene, B. (1996). Sins of omission and commission: Women, psycho-therapy and the psychological literature, *Women & Therapy, 18*(1), 5-31.

Hill-Collins, P. (1998). Toward a new vision: Race, class and gender as categories of analysis and connection. In R. F. Levine (Ed.), *Social class as stratification: Classic statements and theoretical debates* (pp. 231-247). Lanham, MA: Rowman & Littlefield.

Hollingshead, A.B. & Redlich, F. C. (1958). *Social class and mental illness.* New York: John Wiley & Sons.

Mays, V. M. (1985). Black women working together: Diversity in same sex relation-ships. *Women's Studies International Forum, 8,* 67-71.

Mays, V. M., Cochran, S. D., & Rhue, S. (1993). The impact of perceived discrimina-tion on the intimate relationships of Black lesbians. *Journal of Homosexuality 25*(4), 1-14.

Wyche, K. F. (1996). Conceptualizations of social class in African American women: Congruence of client and therapist definitions. *Women & Therapy, 18* (3/4), 35-43.

A Butch Among the Belles

Bonnie R. Strickland

SUMMARY. This memoir of a 65-year-old "butch" lesbian describes her growing-up days in the South and her subsequent professional identity as a university professor and psychologist. The article includes feelings about being raised as a girl while feeling male. Personal reactions to family pressures to conform to a rigid sex role are noted and some attention is given to the effects of living an adult life in the closet. *[Article copies available for a fee from The Haworth Document Delivery Service: 1-800-HAWORTH. E-mail address: <getinfo@haworthpressinc.com> Website: <http://www.HaworthPress. com> © 2002 by The Haworth Press, Inc. All rights reserved.]*

KEYWORDS. Lesbian, butch, femme, sexuality, coming out, narrative

Some societies allow children to determine which sex they prefer or allow them to be both male and female (Feinberg, 1996). In this country we have no choice. When I was born in 1936 in Kentucky, the doctor looked between my legs and pronounced me a girl. This was a great disappointment to my mother,

Bonnie R. Strickland received her PhD in clinical psychology in 1962 from Ohio State University. She is Professor of Psychology at the University of Massachusetts and an active clinician, researcher, and teacher, having published over 100 articles and book chapters. She has been active in various professional associations, including being President of the American Psychological Association.

Address correspondence to: Bonnie R. Strickland, Department of Psychology, University of Massachusetts, Amherst, MA 01003 (E-mail: bonnie@psych.umass.edu).

[Haworth co-indexing entry note]: "A Butch Among the Belles." Strickland, Bonnie R. Co-published simultaneously in *Journal of Lesbian Studies* (Harrington Park Press, an imprint of The Haworth Press, Inc.) Vol. 6, No. 1, 2002, pp. 75-84; and: *Lesbian Love and Relationships* (ed: Suzanna M. Rose) Harrington Park Press, an imprint of The Haworth Press, Inc., 2002, pp. 75-84. Single or multiple copies of this article are available for a fee from The Haworth Document Delivery Service [1-800-HAWORTH, 9:00 a.m. - 5:00 p.m. (EST). E-mail address: getinfo@haworthpressinc.com].

75

who had been told by my father that he wanted a boy. So she kept trying to have a male child, never realizing that she could have stopped with me. My brother arrived four years later, both of us having inherited a particular physical make up from our parents. The circumstances of our births included a genetic and hormonal pattern that led to external genitalia that was female for me and male for him. He grew up happily at home in his body with hormones kicking in at the appropriate times. He assumed himself to be male, as did everyone else around him, including the woman he married and the daughters he raised. In spite of my female genitalia, I grew up a lot like him. I had the same broad shoulders, narrow hips, eventual potbelly and a similar attraction to women. Unlike him, I never felt secure in my gender.

Now I'm certainly not prepared to say that these similarities and differences between my brother and me are only biological. Within our family and our Southern culture, we lived out our own particular dynamics. Growing up, I envied the prerogatives of boys and men and am happy to consider that my gender role may have been primarily developed through social construction and learning. But I am most comfortable believing that each of us is a unique configuration of nature and nurture.

For over sixty years, I have been absorbed with the mystery of my sex and gender, looking for models to assure myself of my identity. First, I was an infant daughter, secure in her mother's arms, later a girl child who felt like a boy. At adolescence, still interested in boyish activities, I found myself attracted to other females. In my young arrogance and fear, I assumed that there was no one else like me and I struggled mightily to understand where I fit across the rigid sexual borders that defined my place in the world of men and women. According to my biological sex, I was female, but I felt masculine across every dimension of my being.

Does one ever escape his or her assigned gender? My earliest memories, whether the events ever occurred or not, are of a beautiful well dressed mother who held me by the hand and took me to have my doll "fixed" at the toy hospital, and a handsome strong father who lifted me into the cab of the train he conducted and let me blow the whistle. There was never a time that I questioned the gender and roles of my parents. My daddy was the strong one, never expressing emotion or concern when my hysterical momma would rage or cry. My momma always seemed to need support and direction from someone, often turning to me for advice when my daddy wasn't available, which was most of the time. I knew that I had to grow up in a hurry, if not to protect her, then at least to protect myself from her. I don't think that my momma really wanted to murder me but she surely couldn't keep me safe. When I was about three or four I was playing in the backyard of my grandmother's home when a bull escaped from his pen and tried to gore me. I was backed against the outside kitchen wall and his horns hit the house on each side of me when he made his first attack. Hearing the house shake, my grandmother ran into the yard waving her apron to scare him off just when he was backing up for his second try, my momma right behind her, crying. Another time, when I was a toddler, my momma took me into a country store. She dropped my hand and I wandered off to a loaded shotgun in the corner, pulled the trigger and shot a hole in the ceiling. At least the gun was pointed straight up. The last "homicide" attempt that I remember was almost a murder-suicide when my momma took me swimming in a public pool, especially in that neither one of us could swim. For whatever reasons, she decided to take me across the deep end, and about halfway across, we both went under and had to be rescued. Maybe she was trying to attract the attention of the handsome lifeguard. I don't know; I do know that at an early age I realized I had to be strong and protect myself. After I grew up and became a psychologist, likely in an attempt to understand these family dynamics, I began to wonder how she really felt about me. I still don't know, but I do suspect that our conflicted relationship led me to look around for other folks who would value and nourish me. Moreover, to keep myself safe, I opted for the alleged active courage of the male rather than the helpless femininity of my momma.

No doubt another strong influence in my growing up was the birth of my brother. My momma brought him home from the hospital and laid him in the middle of the grown-up bed. I stared at his brown eyes and mass of dark, curly hair and asked if he had to stay. With the fierce concern of the four-year-old firstborn, I could feel my world shifting. He now had the bottle that had been mine up until his arrival. But, at a deeper, and more frightening, level, I knew even then that he was the preferred child simply by his being male. I shifted into a homicidal mode, trying to kill him by smothering him while I took the bottle back. My momma protected him, however, with a fury that I doubted she would ever expend on me.

My happy, smiling baby pictures changed after my brother's birth. Although I am still in frilly dresses with ribbons in my hair, I am serious, usually frowning, especially when I am holding him. Was I simply jealous of the second child or was I continually reminded through his presence that as a girl I would now be robbed of boyish pleasures and denied male privilege? In our growing up days, he received the toys that I wanted for Christmas. He was responsible for the fun, outdoor chores like mowing and raking the lawn while I cleaned house and washed dishes. He had the freedom of short hair and long pants while I was relegated to curls and dresses. Even in dresses, though, I played mostly with boys in our made-up war games and pick-up sports. Visiting country cousins, I learned to shoot and hunt and fish with the best of them. I ran the fastest, climbed the highest trees, flexed my biceps and admired my skinny chest. I learned to fight and gloried in competition, regularly beating up my little brother and most everyone else in the neighborhood.

During the World War II years, sex roles were both clear and confusing. Only men could join the armed services, fight in combat, and be killed for their country. On the other hand, my aunt joined the Women's Army Corp and women were taking over men's jobs in the factories and mills. My daddy never had to go into the service since he had an essential war job running the trains, but my male uncles and cousins eagerly joined up. Most of my aunts and female cousins married military men and traveled to various bases while raising their children. The whole country was devoted to the war effort. While the men were fighting, women cheerfully gave up nylons and children gave up bubble gum. We all planted victory gardens and cheered the armed forces in the newsreels of the Saturday matinees. I wanted to grow up and join the Marines, the toughest and, to me, the most heroic of the military branches. I couldn't fathom becoming anything like the female figures associated with the war, Betty Grable, whose name was painted on the bombers that pounded Japan, and Rita Hayworth, whose pictures adorned every barrack.

As I moved through puberty and the country entered the decade of the fifties, sex and gender roles began to emerge with painful clarity. My momma, without explanation, abruptly announced that I could no longer play football with the boys. I was heartbroken. My sense of self had been shaped by competitive sports and the camaraderie of boyhood games. No one cared, especially me, if I was good in girl games such as hopscotch and jump rope, but I was especially proud of having being named center on the 90-lb YMCA boy's football team. Suddenly, I was stripped of whatever was endearing about tomboy activities and had no label or model for who I was. Surrounded by young men and women who knew their assigned roles and even enjoyed them, I felt a deep sense of confusion and difference. At that time, I had no way of knowing that gays and lesbians from the heartland who had found each other during the war years had settled into the ports and cities of both coasts and were building queer communities (Faderman, 1991). However, I did live in a city, Birmingham, Alabama, with public parks and planned activities. I learned to play tennis and eventually became nationally ranked. With our Southern fervor for sports, gender took a backseat to victory and I played on the boy's tennis team of my high school. Moreover, on one lucky day, I wandered over to the softball diamonds at the local park and found a group of women in handsome uniforms playing like professionals. Although too young for the team, I became their groupie, retrieving bats and keeping score. Although I had no label for myself or for these women, I knew that whatever they were called, we were the same.

In high school I dated local boys just like me, especially boys with fast cars. I'm pretty sure that I preferred the cars to the guys. We cruised the drive-ins, drag raced in the streets and spent hours tuning up their cars. Although I tried to engage in the social activities of the working class adolescents of the fifties, my emotional interests were my best girlfriends and the women on the ball teams. Being a voracious reader, I began to look for any information I could find about people like me and finally found a label–sexual pervert. This was no great comfort and didn't seem to fit since I had had little or no sexual experiences of any kind.

Looking back, I realize that my mother was a strong model for me in many ways. She was a single mom when this was unheard of, bought her own home and worked full time to support us kids. For many years, she was a waitress working from 11 a.m. to 11 p.m. six days a week. She ran her own small store for a while, but I thought the best job she ever had was that of department store detective. As I was growing up, our relationship was stormy and distant. I realize now that most of our interactions involved her trying to tell me how to behave as a girl (how to clean house, and dress, and date). I begged to live with my father who seemed benignly indifferent to how I looked or what I did. My momma responded that the day I graduated from high school I could move out on my own. Until then my choice was her home or reform school. I probably should have opted for reform school. I was already imprisoned and, surely, the warden wouldn't have been so obsessively concerned day in and day out as was my mother with forcing me to be female. In her own way, my mother was right. If given my freedom, I would have left her to follow my masculine independence. Indeed, I would have left her for another woman.

Kim Chernin in her book, *My Life as a Boy* (1997), writes:

> If a woman . . . turns into a boy, that may mean that she's having trouble getting out of the place she's in. She requires the instinctive, wholly natural ruthlessness of a boy. He will leave home. Everyone expects it of him. He won't move in next door to his mother or around the block and raise children, not likely. He won't give it a second thought: he's off to see the world, he's a boy, he's going.
>
> I've watched boys take off. I've seen them on bikes, skateboards, motor scooters, sliding on a piece of waxed cardboard. They fly down the middle of the street, cars going fast uphill, downhill, do they care? The direction of a boy is straight out the door, down the hill, out of the neighborhood, into the world. No second thought at leaving people behind, leaving them to fend for themselves as he takes off, hell bent for his own future without them.
>
> I've seen girls on skateboards and girls on waxed cardboard, but I never saw a girl who did not look back and wonder. Not ever. Because there is always someone standing at the door, someone waiting for you to come home, someone who will be happier when they hear your key in the lock. Girls are always aware of this and boys are not.

. . . the fate of a girl, the future she's definitely growing into, holds the certainty of restriction. But for a boy, as I have often observed, there is little danger of becoming a woman. He can be as reckless, as ruthless as he pleases, as carefree, devil-may-care as he likes, breaking his mother's heart, casting off the girl who's waiting for him in the garden. This guy has got to go to sea, and so he's off. (pp. 4-5)

I left like a boy. The week of my high school graduation, I rented a room in a friend's house, packed my few belongings, and moved across town all by myself. I had been working at different jobs since I was 12, always giving my paycheck to my mother, but now I started saving money for myself. In fact, during that summer, I saved so much, about $80 of my $92 monthly paycheck ($8 came out for taxes), that I occasionally went hungry. But work was liberating and my meager pay the first step on a journey toward freedom.

Of course, I had fallen in love with my high school gym teacher. In fact, I had fallen in love with every teacher I had ever had (all women) and am still enthusiastically returning to school each September. But I had a special crush on Mrs. Pope, a delightful, happily married, straight woman who never had children of her own. She took an interest in me, advising me about clothes (she thought I was dressing too boyishly) and signing my report card so I didn't have to show it to my mother. The most important thing she did for me, however, was to give me a model of a strong female figure that could escape a life of early marriage and too many babies too soon. No one in my extended family had ever gone to college; most had never finished high school. Mrs. Pope simply applied to her alma mater for me, arranged for scholarships and quickly sent me off to college before I had a chance to explain that I was supposed to get married and work at some menial job until the babies came.

Although I began Alabama College knowing no one, I was to meet the most dedicated of faculty and the most delightful of women students. I was like a starving kid at a smorgasbord of delicacies that were not food for the body but sustenance for the soul. I attended my first opera, dissected a human cadaver, went on field trips looking for birds and butterflies, and explored underground caves. In contrast to high school, my grades were outstanding–they should have been, I took 90 hours of physical education. I loved college. For the first time, I could follow my interests including doing all sorts of boy-type things, like being cast as the male romantic lead in our school plays or elected captain of our sports teams. I was at home and happy, especially as I came to love women.

During my sophomore year, however, my mother appeared and persuaded the Dean of Women to remove me from my dining hall job, the one that paid the most. She said I was under stress and would become crazy like my father's side of the family. My mother declared that she would pay my expenses and actually did pay a bill of $60. But, as I knew would happen, when the next bill came due, there was no money, save mine, from the jobs she didn't know I had. At that moment, with the clarity of betrayal and rage, I vowed never to depend on anyone for my financial support. Men get jobs, support themselves and others; I would do the same.

Even though I still had no label for myself or for the women to whom I was attracted, I instinctively felt a masculine-feminine dimension with me on the "butch" end. "Butches" were relatively easy to identify with the only term I knew–homosexual, but I was never particularly attracted to them. Rather, I preferred the feminine women whom we might now call "four-year" lesbians or "lugs," lesbians until graduation. They were pretty hard to pick out from the regular straight women but I found them. With few exceptions, the women with whom I had the closest relationships graduated, married and are now happy grandmothers. We made the assumption that being with a woman was a secondary liaison until a man came along. I still remember the agony I felt when I was a bridesmaid in the wedding of a woman I had been sleeping with for two years. Of course, all the same-sex attractions were secretive and guarded. The campus reeled with rumors of expulsion and hospitalization for anyone caught in the "perversion" of Sapphic love. But to my knowledge, our gracious, gentle Dean of Women never threw anyone out for anything.

As I completed my physical education major and prepared to take a job as a gym teacher, one of the psychology faculty, rather like Mrs. Pope, suggested that I apply to graduate school in psychology. Dr. Eber maintained that time in a foreign culture would be more exciting than life in a rural gym and a half-time graduate assistantship would pay as well as full-time schoolteaching. All was settled when he promised that I could always come home if I didn't like it.

No doubt as part of their aid to the culturally deprived, I was accepted in clinical psychology with assistantships at several prestigious universities. Dr. Eber chose Ohio State and, for the first time in my life, I headed north. I did not know one person in the city or the University, although I was quick to learn that I was surrounded by Yankees and, worse yet, Republicans. I began to look around for people like me and actually roomed with a Black Southern woman for a while. Unfortunately for me, she was not romantically interested in women. Surely, there were large numbers of gay men and lesbians but I couldn't find them. There must have been gay bars and clubs but I never learned where they were. Ten years before Stonewall, gay men and lesbians were hidden and homosexuality was still a crime. Some decades later I learned that there had indeed been several other gay men and lesbians in my graduate program. Ironically, in the supposedly liberating process of learning to understand human behavior and help people in need, we were forced to hide our deepest identities and live a life of deception rather than disclosure.

I continued to date men; I like men. When I was growing up I wished that I was one. We have a lot in common, especially our interests in women and cars. In fact, in my wish to live an ordinary and "normal" life, I became engaged to a lovely fellow. We practiced all the routines of the potential newlyweds–an engagement ring, picking out silver, a newspaper announcement. But I never experienced the passion, the excitement, the intimacy that I felt for women and he really wasn't into cars. Realizing that our courtship was more social than sexual, we called off the wedding.

My first faculty position was in Atlanta and I delighted in returning home. I reverted to my first language and reconnected with friends from college. Atlanta was becoming a Mecca for gay men and lesbians from around the South with numerous bars, clubs, sports activities and gay apartment complexes and neighborhoods. Police raids, however, were frequent and frightening, and most lesbians built their communities through personal contacts and private parties. We all lived segregated lives by race, class, and especially sexual orientation. While I was lesbian and butch at home and with gay friends, I was straight and feminine in my job. When I attended social gatherings with my work colleagues, I always had a handsome gay male on my arm, never suggesting that I would rather have a wife than be one. My family and colleagues assumed that I would marry and were continually matching me up with the most unlikely of men while I was dating attractive, feminine lesbian women. I felt like a young Southern gentleman. I drove a Mustang convertible, started an investment portfolio and took luxury vacations; I bought my own home at age 25 and a second beach home by 35. I dated the most popular, beautiful lesbians in town and eventually began a committed relationship with a gorgeous schoolteacher.

When I took a faculty position in New England, my partner left her exceptionally successful coaching career and moved with me. For almost 20 years we were in a prototypical, traditional marriage. I went to work every day and provided our livelihood; she took care of our home. She did the food shopping and prepared the meals. I finally got to mow the lawn and work outside. For most of that time, we were happy but we eventually grew apart, and I suspect that our bland acceptance of stereotypical gender roles was a factor in our break up. In spite of her denials, I think that she really wanted to do more in her life than cook my dinner and entertain for me. We are the best of ex-lovers and, in true gentlemanly fashion, I have been committed to supporting her. She has, however, become a successful businesswoman in her own right and is now the first mate on a yacht that sails from a marina close to her beachfront home. Kind of gives me second thoughts about playing out this "butch" role and working everyday.

Looking back at my "mothers" and mentors, I wonder at how they happened to come along when they did and how they shaped my life. How could Mrs. Pope, for example, have known that Alabama College for Women would be the perfect place for me? Did she instinctively recognize my masculine character, knowing that I would blossom in that unique setting that would allow, even demand, that young women take leadership positions? Did she ever wonder that I would finally be fulfilled in my longing to love other women? I looked to Mrs. Pope throughout my adult life for support and finally confessed to her the details of my life as a lesbian. I visited her regularly in her home in Birmingham, especially after her husband died and she was well into her seventies. Mrs. Pope was a constant in my life. In contrast to my mother who controlled me to keep me close, she encouraged my independence and built bridges for me to cross from ignorance to education, from the dull dead-end of women's work in the fifties to the excitement of professional fulfillment. I thought that she would always be on the other end of the telephone line, the other side of her breakfast table while I was spending a weekend with her. But, about five years ago, I called her home and was told by an operator that the phone had been disconnected with no further information. I called the public schools where she had worked; I went by her empty apartment in Birmingham but I never learned what happened to her. I cried when I didn't receive her Christmas card that year and I cry as I write these words. We never had a chance to say goodbye.

Mrs. Pope took care of me while my birth mother always needed someone to take care of her. I rose to the occasion when necessary, although it was clear that my momma preferred real men. My momma and daddy had fallen in love at first sight and were married three weeks later. Of course, they took a second look and after almost a decade of stormy drama, they divorced. For the next 10 years, from the time I was 7 until I was 17, my momma dated lots of men but always came home to me. After I moved away, she married the man next door the week I entered college and lived with him for almost 10 years. Then she moved to rural northwest Florida to build a house and live on her own. This adventure lasted only as long as it took to dig the well and she married the guy who helped do the plumbing. Eleven years later she left him when she had an opportunity to ride with my Uncle Jennings to my brother's home in South Carolina. Her last liaison of 12 years was with a male friend who died as she was trying to find a nursing home for him.

From the beginning of my life till the end of hers, through all her marriages and liaisons, I assumed that I was supposed to be my mother's keeper. I was the strongest of all of her husbands and my caretaking role became even more consuming as she aged and became frail and demented. Shortly before her death, I brought her to a nursing home in my community. I sat by her bed, with rails to prevent her from falling out, a bed that looked disturbingly like a crib. Without words, her dark eyes searched my face as if to reassure herself that someone still cared that she was here. She likely would have preferred my brother but I treasured our last moments together. My momma had always left her male companions; I was the only one to ever leave her. Now she finally allowed me to return as her child and welcomed me as I held her and tried to comfort her.

After my long term "marriage" collapsed, I found myself single again at age 53 and, as I had at other ages, began looking around for women to date. But life was so different. This was 15 years after Stonewall and I was living in the Pioneer Valley of Massachusetts close to Northampton, often referred to as Lesbianville, USA. The social scene included gay bars, Sunday afternoon Tea Dances, Christmas Balls, softball, women's golf, outdoor adventures, and lesbian newspapers that advertised monthly potlucks for older lesbians to meet each other. The ministers of several of the local churches were lesbians and Christians were marching in the Gay Pride parades. Although I dated a "butch" or two while I was single, I was still clearly attracted to "femmes." Thinking back over my bachelorhood, I realize that most of the women I became involved with were women coming out of straight marriages. My current partner was celebrating her divorce the night I met her. We have been together for four years in what we both believe is a lifelong commitment. She's beautiful, very feminine and, of course, a schoolteacher.

As I finally began to feel comfortable as a butch lesbian, I learned that such roles are politically incorrect and that butch/femme considerations are an historical anomaly. What's an old butch to do? I suspect that we would all be better off if sex roles became less important in our personal identities and each of us was allowed to place ourselves on a continuum wherever we felt most comfortable. But society does not allow us freedom across sex roles and we are forced to make choices that invalidate our very being. I prefer to think of myself as transgendered although that term does not really fit. So I'm happy enough to be a butch lesbian, a label that describes and brings legitimacy and value to who I am. Each of our gender journeys is unique and determined by our culture and our cohort. Mine has crossed boundaries of sexuality, sexual identification, and sexual labels. I feel privileged to have finally found my place with my people.

REFERENCES

Chernin, K. (1997). *My Life as a Boy*. Chapel Hill: Algonquin Books.
Faderman, L. (1991). *Odd Girls and Twilight Lovers*. New York: Columbia Univ. Press.
Feinberg, L. (1996). *Trangendered Warriors*. Boston: Beacon.

Lesbian Dating and Courtship
from Young Adulthood to Midlife

Suzanna M. Rose
Debra Zand

SUMMARY. Lesbian dating and courtship were explored based on interviews with 38 predominantly white lesbians (ages 22-63) representing young adult, adult, and midlife age groups. Friendship was found to be the most widely used courtship script across all age groups, followed by the sexually explicit and romance scripts, with friendship and romance scripts being preferred. Unique aspects of lesbian dating cited by participants included freedom from gender roles, heightened intimacy/friendship, the rapid pace of lesbian relationship development, and the effects of prejudice. Friendship was found to be differentiated from romance by two main criteria: emotional intensity and sexual energy or contact. Verbal declarations of interest and nonverbal behaviors were the primary means of communicating sexual attraction. Few lesbians adhered to traditional gender roles in dating, and those who reported assuming the feminine reactive role nevertheless rejected the traditional notion that

Suzanna M. Rose, PhD, is Professor of Psychology and Director of Women's Studies at Florida International University.

Debra Zand, PhD, is Research Assistant Professor of Psychiatry at the University of Missouri-Columbia. She received her doctorate in clinical psychology in 1997 from the University of Missouri-St. Louis, where she began her research on lesbian relationships.

Address correspondence to: Suzanna M. Rose, PhD, Director, Women's Studies Center, Florida International University, Miami, FL 33199 (E-mail: srose@flu.edu).

Reprinted from *Journal of Gay & Lesbian Social Services*, Vol. 11, No. 2/3, 2000, pp. 77-104. © 2000 by The Haworth Press, Inc. All rights reserved.

[Haworth co-indexing entry note]: "Lesbian Dating and Courtship from Young Adulthood to Midlife." Rose, Suzanna M., and Debra Zand. Co-published simultaneously in *Journal of Lesbian Studies* (Harrington Park Press, an imprint of The Haworth Press, Inc.) Vol. 6, No. 1, 2002, pp. 85-109; and: *Lesbian Love and Relationships* (ed: Suzanna M. Rose) Harrington Park Press, an imprint of The Haworth Press, Inc., 2002, pp. 85-109. Single or multiple copies of this article are available for a fee from The Haworth Document Delivery Service [1-800-HAWORTH, 9:00 a.m. - 5:00 p.m. (EST). E-mail address: getinfo@haworthpressinc.com].

women should limit sexual contact. Overall, midlife lesbians were more purposive in their dating and more free from gender roles. Specifically, they were more concerned about the "attachment-worthiness" of a prospective partner and were significantly more likely than young adults to view dating as having a serious goal, to proceed at a rapid pace, to ask for a date, and to initiate physical intimacy. *[Article copies available for a fee from The Haworth Document Delivery Service: 1-800-HAWORTH. E-mail address: <getinfo@haworthpressinc.com> Website: <http://www.HaworthPress.com>]*

KEYWORDS. Lesbian, midlife, friendship, dating, courtship, gender roles, intimacy, relationship development, sexual attraction

INTRODUCTION

The question "What will we be?" is one of the most exciting, mysterious, and confusing aspects of dating and courtship among lesbians. Will the relationship that has just been initiated result in being lovers, partners, or friends, or some combination? Moreover, exactly how do lesbian relationships typically get initiated? Is dating a clearly defined concept, or is the establishment of contact usually more ambiguous in its intent? These questions are of considerable interest to lesbians. A great many advice and humor books and social commentaries have addressed these issues (e.g., Bechdel, 1997; Eisenbach, 1996; McDaniel, 1995), but a lack of empirical evidence on the topic has ensured that descriptions largely remain anecdotal or speculative.

Our intent in the present research was to provide an in-depth descriptive account of lesbian dating and courtship that would begin to close the gap in knowledge concerning lesbian relationship formation. We examined what courtship scripts lesbians had used in past relationships, how they defined lesbian dating and what was unique about it, and how romantic relations versus friendship were solicited and developed. Also evaluated were the extent to which lesbians adopted gender roles when dating and the impact previous lesbian and heterosexual dating experience had on behavior. Last, a qualitative post hoc analysis was conducted to determine whether developmental changes in views about courtship emerged among the three age groups of participants, including young adult, adult, and midlife lesbians.

Dating and Courtship Scripts

Contemporary (heterosexual) courtship typically relies on dating as a way to initiate romantic relationships (Bailey, 1988). Dating refers to informal interactions with no specific commitment or goal between two individuals with the implied intent of assessing each other's romantic potential (Cate & Lloyd, 1992; Laws & Schwartz, 1977). Although often the labels "dating" and "courtship" are used interchangeably, courtship is a term arising from an earlier era that refers to the system of searching for a mate with whom to make an emotional commitment and enter into a permanent marriage (Cate & Lloyd, 1992). A graduated series of dates is considered the first step to a serious romance (Modell, 1983). Once an exclusive pairing has been established, a couple may enter into a more formal courtship phase.

The extent to which lesbians follow patterns of heterosexual dating and courtship has not been established. That some lesbians date is obvious. Personal advertisements written by lesbians often expressly state an interest in dating. Likewise, lesbians who participated in research by Cini and Malafi (1991) and Klinkenberg and Rose (1994) were able to provide detailed descriptions of dating. However, others declined to participate because they had gotten involved with a friend and never dated. Thus, dating and courtship as they traditionally occur may not apply to lesbians.

Three courtship scripts that have been used by Rose, Zand, and Cini (1993) to describe lesbian couple formation include a romance, friendship, and sexually explicit script. A script refers to a set of stereotypical actions defined by cultural norms that serve as a guide for what feelings and behaviors should occur in a specific situation (Gagnon, 1977; Ginsberg, 1988). The lesbian romance script depicts emotional intimacy and sexual attraction as being intertwined in two women's attraction to each other. The relationship usually rapidly proceeds towards commitment. Dating may be one means of initiating a relationship, but it appears that the dating phase for lesbians may be very short or that a more serious courtship may be preferred from the beginning. For instance, Cini and Malafi (1991) found that by a fifth date, respondents reported being both sexually and emotionally involved and tended to regard themselves as a couple.

In the other two major patterns of lesbian courtship, the friendship script and the sexually explicit script, the components of emotional intimacy and sexual attraction hypothetically play out differently. Neither script requires dating for its initiation. The friendship script, believed to be the most common courtship script among lesbians, emphasizes emotional intimacy over sexuality. According to this script, two women become friends, fall in love, and establish a committed relationship with each other that may or may not be sexual, as in the case of lesbian Boston marriages (e.g., Rothblum & Brehony, 1993). In contrast, the sexually explicit script primarily focuses on sexuality and attraction; emotional intimacy is less important or may not even be present. In this script, two women who are physically attracted to each other purposefully initiate sexual contact with no implied goal of future commitment. The most immediate questions raised by the preceding discussion are: What courtship scripts do lesbians actually use, and what script is most preferred? Related issues concern how lesbians define dating and whether lesbian dating has unique characteristics not associated with heterosexual models. These were addressed in the present research. In addition, the degree to which scripts may overlap may create ambiguity. The courtship scripts described above may not be as distinct in practice as in theory. The friendship script is one that is particularly confusing, because it is often difficult for lesbians to know whether an informal interaction with another woman is a date or a non-romantic friendship overture. What script is followed may be easier to discern in retrospect than during its enactment. If the pair becomes a couple, they later may tend to classify the interaction as a date/romance script; if not, it may be seen as just getting together as friends. The motives of the two women involved also might differ, with one assuming they are "just friends" and the other assuming it is a date. Or, scripts might be blended, with both friendship and romance as the goal. Lesbians place a high value on friendship and appear to act quickly to establish an intimate connection within the context of a dating relationship (Rose et al., 1993). Two questions raised by script ambiguity that also were explored in the present research concerned how lesbians distinguish friendship from romance and what rituals signal the progression of the relationship to a more serious level, such as from friendship or dating to commitment.

Gender Roles and Courtship

The impact of gender roles on lesbian courtship also was investigated in the present research. First, it was expected lesbians would use more indirect than direct means of communicating interest in a partner. Traditional gender roles prescribe that men initiate the relationship; women are expected to wait to be asked for a date. As women, lesbians may not have been socialized to initiate dating or courtship. This is perhaps one reason lesbians have been described as notoriously inactive in approaching another woman in whom they are interested (e.g., DeLaria, 1995; Sausser, 1990). For instance, Jacqueline Lapidus (1995) labeled the non-initiating style of lesbian dating she practiced "procrasti-dating." In addition, although the direct initiation of contact in heterosexual interactions is traditionally the man's prerogative, research on nonverbal behavior indicates that women actually may do the choosing by signaling a partner to approach them using "proceptive behaviors" such as a darting glance, moving close, or touching (e.g., Perper & Weis, 1987; Moore, 1985). What is perceived as male choice may be, in fact, the final step of a selection and artful solicitation by the woman using eye contact, positive facial expressions, smiling, laughing, and light touch. Thus, as women, lesbians may be especially skilled at sending and interpreting nonverbal cues. Subsequently, we predicted that lesbians would rely on nonverbal proceptive behaviors more than direct verbal approaches (e.g., asking for a date) to convey romantic interest.

Second, based on gender socialization, we predicted that lesbians would prefer the friendship script over the romance or sexually explicit scripts. For instance, the need for one woman to assume the traditional male role of initiator in dating relationships may be circumvented by the friendship script. Women also generally are socialized to value intimacy and expressiveness over sexuality in relationships, a pattern of interaction that is most compatible with the friendship script. Moreover, the process of coming out occurs within the context of a friendship for many lesbians (e.g., Grammick, 1984).

Third, although heterosexuals' dating scripts have been shown to adhere strongly to gender roles, particularly among experienced daters, with men assuming an active role and women a reactive one (Rose & Frieze, 1989; 1993), lesbians were not expected to follow suit. When dating, lesbians tend not to assign the active role to one person, instead preferring to share the responsibility for orchestrating the date (Klinkenberg & Rose, 1994). In other words, lesbians typically behave consistently with gender roles, that is, most do not adopt the male role. The prediction that few lesbians would adopt heterosexual roles was explored in the present research by asking participants the extent to which they assumed either a traditional masculine role when dating (i.e., asking for a date, planning it, picking her up, performing courtly behaviors such as holding doors open, paying for the date, and initiating sexual contact), or a feminine role (i.e., waiting to be asked for a date, and allowing or refusing sexual advances). Previous heterosexual and lesbian dating experience also was assessed in order to test whether dating experience affected gender role behavior.

In summary, it appears that an exploration of lesbian dating and courtship would be a fruitful place to begin the study of lesbian relationship initiation. In the present research, the four issues raised above were investigated, including: (a) what courtship scripts lesbians used and preferred; (b) how lesbians defined dating, including what was unique about it; (c) how romantic relations were distinguished from friendship, including how they are solicited and progress; and (d) the extent to which lesbians adopted gender roles and how previous dating experience affected roles.

Developmental Issues

Whether courtship among lesbians is affected by adult development remains an open question. On the one hand, courtship scripts might be quite robust and show little variation over the life span. For example, scripts for a first date among both young heterosexual adults in their 20s and lesbians and gay men in their 20s and 30s were found to be quite similar, suggesting that compliance with cultural norms occurs across age and is particularly likely at the early stage of a relationship (Klinkenberg & Rose, 1994; Rose & Frieze, 1989; 1993).

In contrast, the little information we have about lesbians' adult development suggests that notions of dating and courtship may be affected by age. Key developmental tasks for adolescent and young adult lesbians include coming out and establishing an intimate relationship (Savin-Williams, 1995). Rose (1996) has suggested that lesbians entering their first relationship may be particularly likely to adopt a friendship script because cultural scripts for same-sex romance are not widely available. Thus, a same-sex attraction initially may be labeled or encoded as friendship rather than attraction. In young adulthood, lesbians also may lack opportunities to learn or apply other scripts due to confusion about their sexual identity, lack of role models, lack of same-age partners, or fear of anti-lesbian violence from peers (Savin-Williams, 1995). Even so, many lesbians establish their first serious relationship in their 20s.

Research on adult (30-39 years) and midlife (40-65) lesbians largely has been aimed at understanding couple relationships rather than courtship. This research emphasis reflects the heterosexist linearity of life span and relationship research, which assumes that young adult courtship will be followed by lifelong monogamy. Although often not true for heterosexuals today, this linearity may be even less applicable to lesbians for several reasons. First, although many lesbians aspire to the cultural norm of establishing a lifelong monogamous relationship with a partner, few achieve this during their early adulthood, as is prescribed by traditional values. Instead, there is a strong likelihood that lesbians may have several episodes of same-sex dating, courtship, and partnership in their lifetimes. Available research indicates that a majority of lesbians in their thirties have had at least one previous lesbian relationship (Bryant & Demian, 1990). At midlife, most lesbians in committed partnerships have had more than one previous significant relationship and a substantial proportion (33 to 43 percent) are single (Bradford & Ryan, 1991; Hall & Gregory, 1991; Sang, 1991). Second, not all lesbians endorse the concept of lifelong monogamy. West (1996) has contended that a substantial proportion of lesbians–about one in five–practice polyfidelity, that is, they are openly romantically and/or sensually involved with more than one woman concurrently. Thus, we expected to find that many lesbians would be actively dating and courting well beyond their 20s.

By midlife (40-65), it is possible to speculate based on limited information that developmental changes in dating and courtship might occur in a few areas. Lesbians between the ages of 40 and 60 have a strong sense of self as a consequence of establishing an identity separate from others and proving themselves as independent persons during their early adulthood (Kimmel & Sang, 1995). Subsequently, they may adhere less to gender roles. Because most lesbians work from economic necessity, work continues to be a strong part of their identity. However, lesbians persist in deeply valuing relationships all their lives, often wanting more time at midlife to enjoy partners, friends, and personal interests. Lesbian couples often follow a "best friend" model in their relationships that promotes equality (Rose & Roades, 1987). Friends play a particularly strong role in the lives of both coupled and single lesbians. Lesbian friends around the same age, often including ex-lovers, constitute one of the greatest sources of support for a majority of midlife lesbians (Bradford & Ryan, 1991). In addition, for at least some midlife lesbians, the idea that they would live "forever after" with one partner has been tempered by their experience (Hall & Gregory, 1991). Thus, midlife lesbians may approach dating and courtship with more maturity. For instance, they may have used more courtship scripts, developed clearer preferences for how and what kind of relationship they wish to establish, be more skilled at interpreting or signaling romantic interest, and be less affected by gender expectations.

The pattern of adult development is affected further by social age norms, historical effects, and idiosyncratic transitions (Kimmel & Sang, 1995). Lesbians who enter their first courtship today face an immensely improved social climate compared to those who came out decades ago. How these different experiences interact with age to affect dating and courtship remains to be determined.

Overall, the multiplicity of influences on dating and courtship for lesbians across the life span makes developmental changes difficult to predict. Not enough groundwork has yet been laid in terms of lesbian adult development or cohort effects to anticipate reliably how dating might be affected. Thus, our intent in the present research was to investigate how and why lesbians date, without specifically focusing on developmental issues. However, a qualitative post hoc analysis of lesbian dating was undertaken to determine whether developmental changes could be identified. To that end, responses from 38 lesbians we interviewed were examined as a function of three age groups, including young adults (20-29), adults (30-39), and midlife (40-65).

In summary, the research on lesbian dating and courtship presented here was intended to provide an exploratory descriptive analysis of lesbian relationship formation. Intensive interviews were conducted with lesbians to obtain the answer to 12 questions addressing the following themes: what courtship scripts were used, how dating was defined, how romantic relationships versus friendships were solicited and developed, and what impact gender roles and previous experience had on dating. The impact of adult development on dating and courtship for lesbians at three stages of life also was examined.

METHOD

Participants

The sample consisted of 38 lesbians between the ages of 22 to 63 years ($M =$ 35.9, $SD = 10.5$). All participants were recruited at lesbian and gay community events or through friendship networks in a large midwestern city. The group studied was mostly white and middle class as determined by education and income. Ninety-two percent were white and 8% were African-American. The mean educational level of the participants was 17 years with a range of 12 to 21 years. The average income of participants was $22,687 with a range of $5,000 to $58,000. Most lesbians (89%) currently were involved in a committed relationship with another woman.

The age groups represented by participants included young adults (20-29 years; $N = 13$), adults (30-39 years; $N = 12$), and midlife adults (40-65 years; $N = 13$). The education and income of the sample are reported by age group in Table 1. Mean scores for the following variables also are included in Table 1: number of years as a lesbian, number and length of previous romantic relationships, length of current relationship, and amount of lesbian and heterosexual dating experience. Analyses of variance indicated that adult and midlife lesbians earned significantly more than young lesbians and had embraced a lesbian identity longer. Mean length of romantic relationships (excluding current relationship) also was significantly longer for adult and midlife lesbians than young adults.

Measures

An interview consisting of 12 open-ended questions was administered to all participants. Age, race, income and other demographic information also was obtained. In addition, participants were asked to evaluate the extent of their lesbian and heterosexual dating experiences on a five-point scale ranging from 1 = no experience to 5 = extensive experience. Last, participants rated the frequency with which they engaged in eight gender role behaviors (e.g., asks for date, pays for activities) found by Rose and Frieze (1989) to be highly stereotyped on first dates for heterosexuals (5-point scale, 5 = occurs frequently).

Procedure

The second author interviewed all participants in their homes. Interviews took approximately 15 minutes to three hours to complete; median interview length was 45 minutes. All interviews were tape recorded and transcribed.

TABLE 1. Characteristics of Lesbian Participants by Age Group

Characteristic	Young Adulthood (20-29 yrs.) (N = 13) %	M	SD	Early Midlife (30-39 yrs.) (N = 12) %	M	SD	Later Midlife (40-65 yrs.) (N = 12) %	M	SD
Race									
White	100			75			100		
African-American	0			25			0		
Relationship status									
Single	15			8			8		
Coupled	85			92			92		
Relationship length		1.9	(2.2)		4.8	(4.2)		5.4	(4.3)
Education		17.0	(1.4)		16.7	(1.3)		6.2	(2.5)
Income		14K	(9K)		24K	(12K)		27K	(14K)[a]
Years as a lesbian		8.1	(5.2)		16.3	(3.9)		14.8	(7.2)[b]
Number previous relationships		3.5	(2.6)		4.8	(2.1)		3.6	(2.4)
Length of previous relationships (yrs.)[c]		1.8	(2.4)		3.1	(2.9)		4.6	(3.6)
Dating experience[d]									
Lesbian		2.8	(1.2)		3.2	(1.1)		3.2	(1.3)
Heterosexual		2.8	(1.1)		2.4	(0.8)		3.3	(1.2)

[a]Adult and midlife groups earned significantly more, $F(2,27) = 4.36$, $p \leq .03$.
[b]Adult and midlife groups had been lesbians significantly longer, $F(2,27) = 4.44$, $p \leq .03$.
[c]Adult and midlife groups had significantly longer previous relationship than younger adults $F(2,35) = 3.09$, $p \leq .06$.
[d]5-point scale, 5 = extensive experience

Coding

A coding system consisting of 48 categories was used to classify responses to the 12 open-ended questions. The categories were generated from a content analysis of the transcripts. Individual statements then were coded as belonging to specific categories. The reliability of assignment of statements to a coding category was 83%; this percentage represents the frequency of agreement between two raters who independently scored 25% of the transcripts.

RESULTS AND DISCUSSION

Courtship Experience and Scripts

Participants had considerable courtship experience. As shown in Table 1, on average, lesbians had 3 to 4.6 previous romantic relationships, in addition to their current relationship. Thus, most had from 4 to 6 relationships as a basis for describing their courtship script usage. The use of courtship scripts was assessed by reviewing each transcript to determine whether respondents had ever engaged in the romance, friendship, or sexually explicit script. About 29% of participants had used all three scripts, 47% had used two, and 29% had used only one.

As predicted, the results indicated that the friendship script was the most widely used. About 74% of lesbians reported having been friends with a woman, on at least one occasion, before becoming romantically involved with her. In comparison, 55% had used the romance script and 63% had engaged in a sexually explicit script. An example of each script taken from participant transcripts is presented in Table 2. Script preference followed a slightly different pattern, however, with half of the lesbians preferring the friendship script and half preferring the romance script across all age groups. None of the participants indicated a preference for the sexually explicit script, despite the prevalence of its use.

The most used script, friendship, generally proceeded according to the following schema. A friendship was established between two women who highly valued the emotional intimacy of their connection. The intimacy and companionship of the friendship gradually led the women to a deep emotional commitment that was expressed physically as well. The motive for establishing a

TABLE 2. Examples of Courtship Scripts Classified as Friendship, Romance, or Sexually Explicit

---

Friendship Script

We had known each other for nine years in total, and we've been a couple for almost seven of those years. We had a really strong foundation as friends. We drank together and went to the movies together. It made some foundation for a relationship. There was not that intense physical part that came all at once. I was interested in her and she had been interested in me, but neither one of us knew about the other's lesbianism. *(A 25-year-old lesbian)*

Romance Script

We started out dating. It wasn't like we had been friends first. After we saw each other for a few times, she said she wanted to be more than friends. Then she was expecting me to spend more time with her. It was difficult because I had four kids, school, and work, but we found that time. I started to feel like [we were] a couple after about a month. It kind of reminds me of the old joke, "Friday night you go out, Monday, you're married, and Tuesday, you make the appointment with the therapist." *(A 42-year-old lesbian)*

Sexually Explicit Script

I was out of town at the time. It was at a low point in my first relationship and I went traveling for a little while to San Francisco with my gay buddy. We went to a bar and there was a woman coming on to me and my friend said, "Go for it." I thought, "OK, since you are insisting." We had a great time. We essentially had a long weekend. After that, I wasn't interested. *(A 51-year-old lesbian)* friendship before getting romantically involved varied. For some, a friendship was developed first because one (or both) was unaware of her lesbianism. In other cases, the women were aware of their sexual attraction but were constrained from acting on it because one was in a serious relationship with someone else.

Although the friendship script had been used by a majority of lesbians (72%), the finding that it was preferred by fewer (50%) suggests this script may have some drawbacks. One disadvantage that was mentioned by a number of lesbians was the script's ambiguity. As one participant (age 33) explained:

> The thing that really gets cloudy in lesbian relationships for me is that I tend to fall in love with best friends–a person you would be able to confide in or go to dinner with or share secrets with or just to share a good time with. And if I'm close enough to that person, I'm going to find a love relationship and be attracted. That's where it gets real cloudy. Once I embraced a lesbian identity, it seems the people that I am best friends with wind up becoming a partner.

Even so, those who preferred the friendship script frequently did so because they believed it led to a more secure basis for a permanent commitment.

The romance script, the preferred courtship script of half of participants, had two major characteristics, including an emotional intensity and a conscious sexual attraction between the two women. The pair often began by dating or flirting with each other and, occasionally, by being fixed up on a blind date by a friend. The development of an intimate friendship, often forged by long hours on the telephone or many lengthy one-on-one conversations, combined with a strong physical attraction, quickly led to overt sexual contact. Being sexual, in turn, enhanced the couple's emotional bond. For many, becoming sexual also served as a "marker" that signified they were a couple.

One reason given for preferring the romance script was participants' emotional and physical enjoyment of the seduction. The seduction was seen as being both playful and exciting. As one lesbian (age 35) described it:

> I am the one who made the first physical move in my current relationship, and that usually is not the case. But [one night] she had this lounging appearance, with her arms up behind her head, in a kind of daring position, like, "Come over here and kiss me. I dare you." There was a playful energy between us as to which one of us was going to make the first move. So, she had kind of set the stage for it, and it was up to me to go ahead with it or not. So I did. It was fun!

A second reason given for preferring a romance script was that some individuals made a clear distinction between sexual attraction and friendship and tended not to be sexually attracted to their friends. However, some of those who rejected the romance script specifically mentioned feeling uncomfortable with sexual play and seduction.

Responses classified as fitting the sexually explicit script strongly emphasized physical attraction over other aspects of the interaction. Of the 63% of respondents who had engaged in this script at least once, most had initiated the relationship at bars (46%), followed by parties (13%), ads in lesbian/gay newspapers (8%), work settings (4%), and public places (4%). A typical script involved two women meeting, being aware of a mutual sexual attraction, acting on it, and either parting ways immediately or after a relationship of relatively short duration (e.g., a few weeks or months). For instance, one woman (age 25) indicated, "On three different occasions, I went into a bar, got to know a few people there, had drinks with a woman, and went home with her. It was very casual. Just a convenient couple of weeks resulted. No long-term relationship."

Evaluations of the sexually explicit script by participants were mixed. Some felt it had been a negative experience. "It was obviously lust at first sight," a 30-year-old lesbian explained. "Before I knew it, we had gotten involved and we hadn't established any kind of friendship. That was a disaster. We had a relationship for a few turbulent months." However, positive outcomes, including the development of a friendship or romantic relationship, were cited by 58% of participants who had used this script, for example:

> I was at a conference. I was involved in a lot of grassroots organizations in various cities and she is someone I met at a conference. She had come in late, and there wasn't any room for her with the party she was staying with. I said, "We can fix this." We went home and didn't sleep all night. I heard from her several times after that. It then became more of a friendship. We lost touch after about 10 years. (a 36-year-old)

In summary, most young adult, adult, and midlife lesbians had participated in several successful courtships. A majority had used the friendship script at least once, but many also used the romance and sexually explicit scripts. However, lesbians were split about equally in their preference for friendship versus romance scripts, whereas the sexually explicit script was not endorsed by anyone as a preferred script. These results show that lesbians are versatile in their use of courtship scripts and, as expected, that issues concerning courtship are salient to lesbians throughout the life span.

Lesbian Dating and Uniqueness

Questions about whether lesbian dating existed and what was unique about it were asked to determine how much lesbians conformed to traditional views of dating. Three responses to the question of whether lesbian dating existed were obtained. Those who replied "yes," indicating they had dated in the past, were in the majority (63%). They defined dating as being a way to get to know another woman and have a good time or to explore the romantic or sexual potential of the relationship without any specific commitment in mind. This definition parallels the modern one of (heterosexual) dating as involving informal, unchaperoned, male-female interaction with no specific commitment (Murstein, 1974). One lesbian (age 23) described dating as "like what the traditional American teenager considers a date . . . I've had women call me up and say 'Would you like to go to the movies? I'll pick you up.' And they bring flowers and all that jazz." Dating was described variously as providing a chance "to go out and see what it is all about before you hop into bed or move in with somebody," "to get to know someone before you have them in your apartment," and "to pursue an interest in another woman in a social context." One woman (age 23) offered the advice, "I agree with a gay man friend of mine who says, 'The first two months that you go out with somebody, you shouldn't have any real deep conversations. You should just have fun.' "

The second most common response to the question of whether lesbian dating exists, endorsed by 24% of participants, was to assert that courting, rather than dating, was the correct term to use. Midlife lesbians comprised the majority of participants in this group. Courting implied a more serious purpose than dating; establishing a permanent partnership was the goal. For instance, one 46-year-old woman indicated, "I prefer [the term] 'courting.' 'Dating' is not a courting process. In my experience, courting has always been [for the purpose of] getting to know the person for a potential lifetime commitment." Another lesbian (age 60) said, "Yes, dating exists [among lesbians], but minimally . . . Unlike heterosexuals, lesbians get seriously involved more immediately instead of having a trial or dating experience. That's been my experience." "There is dating, but it is difficult dating," explained another (age 41). "We [older lesbians] tend to get very territorial, and I think that's because there are so few of us. We're like the dinosaurs–a dying breed."

The remaining 13% of participants, distributed about equally across age groups, said they had never dated and believed that dating did not exist among lesbians. These women had established all their romantic relationships via a friendship. "I never felt I was dating," indicated one lesbian (age 45). "I felt that I was going out with a friend and that we were building something greater than friendship." "I don't know if I've ever dated," claimed another (age 29).

"For me, it has been kind of a mutual discovery process." Similarly, one (age 36) explained, "It has always been more knowing someone and at some point becoming attracted to them and moving from there. The period of dating isn't there." The diversity of definitions provided above suggest that cultural norms based on heterosexual dating enjoyed limited acceptance among the lesbians we interviewed. Responses to the question "What is unique about lesbian dating?" provided further evidence that lesbian dating did not conform to a heterosexual model. Only 23% to 31% reported that there was nothing unique about lesbian dating. (See Table 3.) The remaining participants cited four major categories of uniqueness, including freedom from gender roles, heightened

TABLE 3. Descriptions of What Is Unique About Lesbian Dating by Category of Response and Age Group

Category of Response	Examples	Percentage Responding by Age Group[a]		
		Young Adult (N = 13)	Adult (N = 12)	Midlife (N = 13)
Not anything unique	It [lesbian dating] follows the heterosexual model. Someone has to adopt the male role.	31	33	23
Freedom from gender roles	One person is not in control; the roles are less defined. It's not clear who initiates.	38	25	38
Heightened intimacy/ friendship	The friendship develops as well as the sexual part. I'm more comfortable with women; I can be myself.	23	17	15
Rapid pace of relationship	Women are just ready to move in. A date could last for days and be a really intense experience.	15	0	54[b]
Effects of prejudice	There are limits on where you can go and what you can do. The need to conceal or explain the relationship.	7	25	31
Other	You can lose the friendship if being lovers doesn't work out. It's hard to know if it [the date] is a friend thing or a date thing.	15	8	7

[a]Columns do not add to 100% due to multiple responses.
[b]Midlife lesbians differ significantly from other two age groups, $X^2(2) = 9.99, p \leq .01$.

intimacy/friendship, the rapid pace of lesbian relationship development, and the effects of prejudice. A fifth category, other, was used to classify miscellaneous responses mentioned only once.

The characteristics "freedom from gender roles" and "heightened intimacy" suggest that lesbian dating is more egalitarian than heterosexual dating. Behaviors usually associated with the masculine role, such as who initiates and pays, were usually shared. The interaction also appeared to be less geared toward trying to impress the other person by spending money, doing courtly behaviors such as opening doors, or worrying about appearance, and more towards genuinely getting to know each other. Participants also pointed out that societal prejudice against lesbians placed limits on how openly they could date.

Significantly more midlife lesbians (54%) cited the rapid pace of relationship development as a distinctive feature of lesbian dating compared to the young adult (15%) or adult group (0), χ^2 (2) = 9.99, $p \leq .01$. As one woman (age 41) explained, "the shortness of it [is unique]. You immediately find yourself in a lot more serious relationship than what you might want." Another (age 46) elaborated, "[Lesbians] get involved really quickly and then think of themselves as being in a relationship and not dating anymore. That means they live together; they're in a partnership." There are at least two possible explanations for the finding that midlife lesbians view the rapid pacing of relationships as unique. First, due to age and experience, midlife lesbians may have different values and expectations for relationships. For instance, they may be more clear about what they are looking for in a partner or be less willing to spend time in casual interactions than younger lesbians. Subsequently, they may go out with someone only if they feel there is a strong possibility for the relationship to develop. This interpretation is partially supported by findings described earlier showing that many midlife lesbians favor the term "courtship" over "dating," to signify that their goal was to establish a long-term relationship. Alternatively, midlife lesbians may have fewer available partners from which to choose. If so, the resulting anxiety about finding a companion among those who desire one may cause them to escalate the course of the relationship. Two midlife lesbians supported this interpretation by contending that it was extremely rare to find a single lesbian in the 40 to 65 age group and that, if they found one, they would feel considerable pressure to pursue her. However, more research would be required to accurately explain why midlife lesbians saw the rapid pacing of lesbian relationships as unique more so than younger ones.

In summary, dating was viewed as an informal interaction with no goal of commitment across all age groups by a majority of lesbians, most of whom had dated. However, "courtship" and "friendship" were two alternatives to dating that were preferred by some. Lesbian dating was described as being relatively free from gender roles, intimate, and quick to develop. Constraints on dating due to societal prejudice against lesbians also were noted. Midlife lesbians differed from younger lesbians in two important areas: (a) they were more likely to be seeking a serious commitment when dating or courting, and (b) they were more likely to view lesbian relationships as proceeding at a fast pace. These findings indicate that midlife lesbians may approach dating and courtship with different expectations.

Friendship versus Romance

Three questions were asked in the present research to explore how romantic relationships develop between lesbians: (a) What distinguishes a friendship from a romantic relationship? (b) What signifies to you that a change in relationship status [to being a couple] has occurred? (c) How do you let a woman know that you are interested in her romantically or know she is interested in you?

Confusion about whether a friendly versus a romantic interest motivates interactions between lesbians is a common phenomenon. One challenge for lesbians is to interpret whether friendly interest has the potential to develop into sexual attraction or is consciously or unconsciously motivated by it. In terms of distinguishing a friendship from a romance, five lesbians (13%) maintained that there was no distinction between the two. They only became partners with friends and saw the sexual aspects of the relationship as being an extension of a deep emotional commitment to the friendship. A majority (87%), however, used two main characteristics to discriminate between friendship and romance. Of these, 58 percent described friendships as being both less emotionally intense (for example, "don't invest as much emotional energy," "less tension," "talk about surface things") and lacking in sexual energy or contact. Participants also indicated being more direct about their intentions (25%) and more relaxed with friends (21%) than with potential lovers.

Lesbians may find it difficult to discern if or when a friendship has moved "over the line" into a romance. They also must create their own "markers" for transitions in their relationships due to lack of access to public rituals of commitment such as engagement and marriage. A majority of the lesbians we interviewed (68%) regarded the presence of sexual energy or contact as marking a change in status from friendship to romance. Sexual desire or behavior signaled that the relationship had become "more than friendship." Other indicators of a change in status that were commonly cited included: increased emotional closeness (40%), verbal declarations of love or commitment (37%), and living together or buying a house together (29%). On average, it took six months for this change to occur, with a range of two weeks to two years. Markers varied for many depending on the relationship, for example:

It's been different with everybody. I've gone from knowing it's leading that way because we became more serious and gradually spent more time together–to waking up one morning and finding that all her clothes were there and she had moved in. With one woman, I realized we were a couple when every plant that she owned was in my house. I woke up one morning and had a house full of green stuff and her. I thought, "Oh, wow, I guess she's gonna stay." (a 41-year-old)

Lastly, how lesbians convey and interpret sexual attraction is an interesting question, given neither woman is likely to have been socialized to assume the initiator role. One current stereotype about lesbians is that they approach dating and courtship passively, like sheep; that is, they wait to be asked out and to be pursued sexually (Rose et al., 1993). Based on this stereotype, we predicted that lesbians would tend not to favor a direct verbal approach. This prediction was supported for two categories of behavior, including "asking for a date," and "waiting to be asked for a date." Relatively few lesbians indicated they had directly asked another woman for a date. (See Table 4.) In addition, 50% indicated on the gender role measure that they "always" or "almost always" waited to be asked for a date.

However, contrary to expectation, a majority of lesbians used direct verbal declarations to convey and read romantic interest (e.g., "tell her how I feel," "proposition her sexually," and "declare my affection"). This suggests that lesbians are far from shy in terms of signaling attraction. The second most frequently cited category of sexual signaling was the use of nonverbal proceptive behaviors. As expected, lesbians relied heavily on the nuances of touching,

TABLE 4. Percentage of Participants (*N* = 38) Citing Behaviors that Convey Attraction

Behavior	Definition	Percentage Citing Used by Self	Used by Partner
Ask for a date	Invite to an activity	18	16
Direct statements	Verbal declaration of interest	79	74
Nonverbal cues	Touching, smiling, eye contact	45	66
Attentiveness	Sexual energy, listening to partner, intuition	40	42
Indirect	Draw attention to self indirectly	18	13
Nothing	No behavioral displays	3	8

smiling, and maintaining eye contact to convey interest, behaviors that were described in elegant detail by many participants. The finding in Table 4 that more lesbians depended on nonverbal signals to decipher interest than they did to signal interest might imply for some a reticence to assume an active role. Alternatively, it may indicate simply that more lesbians are aware of the other woman's behavior than their own in a romantic situation. Attentiveness to the partner was the third most often mentioned means of signaling attraction. Attentiveness was defined as actively giving their attention by listening or being attuned to the needs of their prospective partners. Indirect means of attracting a partner, such as "showing off" or "telling a mutual friend," were cited by only a small percentage. An even smaller number insisted that they engaged in no behavioral displays of interest.

One age difference was observed for the measure "ask for a date." Significantly more young adult lesbians than adult or midlife lesbians said they always or almost always waited to be asked for a date, χ^2 (2) = 11.7, $p < .005$. Conversely, older lesbians were more likely to have asked someone for a date. It is reasonable to speculate that, as lesbians age, they may move farther away from the traditional feminine role, or they may become comfortable adopting either role depending on the occasion.

These findings challenge the stereotype of lesbians as being passive when it comes to approaching another woman. Many participants were quite sophisticated about the process of seduction. One lesbian (age 38) described her sexual signaling system as follows:

> [If I wanted to show a woman I was interested], I would let her know by letting my sexual energy be felt–to let it flow. [That means] I would be relaxed around her and be more myself, which means that she is going to feel a sense of my sexuality, as opposed to being around someone straight or a friend. I would be perceptive about her nonverbal language. She may make slight innuendoes. I can tell if she's interested by the way she waits for my responses to the cues that she gives me. She may lean forward when I am talking as opposed to looking off to the side. A lot of eye contact. Light touching usually happens. A softness to her voice. Her voice tone may change to being a slower paced rate of speaking, maybe with a little sexy edge to it. Her voice may drop. It is definitely not a normal speaking tone. That is a sure indication of her attraction. [To convey attraction] I would use more direct types of touching. Maybe my full hand on her arm or a couple of fingers on her leg. Legs tend to be more sexual. It's hard to give a formula. It just depends on my mood, how

much I like the person, her style as it meshes with mine. It depends on so many different things.

The results concerning how romantic relationships progress suggest that lesbians have been creative in coping with the ambiguity of the friendship script, have developed markers for relationship transitions that are based primarily on sexual and emotional intimacy, and are verbally and nonverbally expressive about their attractions during courtship. Evidence that young lesbians are more tied to gender roles in terms of asking for a date than older lesbians also implies that age may be related to greater flexibility in dating.

Gender Roles and Dating Experience

A majority of lesbians (55%) rejected gender roles by either mutually negotiating their interactions or switching roles depending on the specific interaction. Others opted more consistently for a particular role as either the initiator (16%) or noninitiator (29%).

Correlational analyses were conducted on ratings of gender-role behaviors to determine if lesbians' assumption of a role paralleled that of heterosexual roles. Behaviors associated with the traditional masculine role were significantly related. How often a lesbian asked for a date was found to be positively related to how often she picked her date up (r (33) = .51, $p < .001$); planned the date (r (31) = .36, $p < .02$); did courtly behaviors during the date, such as buying flowers, giving compliments, and holding doors open (r (33) = .43, $p < .006$); paid for the date (r (33) = .34, $p < .023$); and initiated physical intimacy on the date (r (32) = .35, $p < .024$). Thus, it appeared that if a lesbian initiated a date, she also assumed other aspects of the traditional male role.

Conversely, lesbians who waited to be asked for a date were significantly unlikely to pick up the date (r (34) = $-.39$, $p < .05$); plan it (r (32) = $-.54$, $p < .01$); do courtly behaviors (r (34) = $-.36$, $p < .05$); or initiate physical intimacy (r (33) = $-.48$, $p < .01$). However, waiting to be asked for a date did *not* correlate with ratings for the item, "turned down physical intimacy," a behavior that traditionally has been assigned to heterosexual women (e.g., Peplau, Rubin, & Hill, 1977). What these findings suggest is that lesbians who assume the feminine reactive role in dating, unlike heterosexual women, do not play a restrictive role in terms of limiting sexual contact.

Previous research has demonstrated a relationship between dating experience and gender roles, with more experienced heterosexual daters engaging in more stereotypical behavior (Rose & Frieze, 1989). The impact of lesbian and heterosexual experience on ratings of the eight gender role behaviors was examined using analysis of variance to test for mean differences between inexperienced daters (i.e., those with ratings of 1 or 2 on a 5-point scale) and experienced ones (i.e., ratings of 4 or 5 on the scale). Experienced lesbian daters were found to have initiated physical intimacy on their dates ($M = 3.19$) significantly more often than those with little lesbian dating experience ($M = 1.93$), $F (1,28) = 6.84$, $p < .02$. Lesbian dating experience was not significantly related to other gender behaviors. Those with extensive heterosexual dating experience were found to reject physical intimacy more often ($M = 2.66$) than those with little experience ($M = 1.83$), $F (1,30) = 5.83$, $p < .02$; no other effects were found.

Last, the relationship between age and the "initiate physical intimacy" measure was explored. Adult and midlife lesbians were found to be significantly more likely to have initiated sexual behavior ($M = 3.00$ and 2.87, respectively) than young adult lesbians ($M = 1.82$), $F (2,32) = 3.24$, $p < .05$.

In sum, the findings concerning gender roles and dating experience suggest that lesbian dating experience enables women to freely initiate sexual interactions, whereas heterosexual dating experience reinforces the role of the woman as the sexual "limit setter." Thus, it appears that the use of gender roles as practiced by lesbians does not dictate sexual interactions. Also, as lesbians get older and have more lesbian dating experience, they appear to become more comfortable with initiating sexual intimacy.

Age and Courtship

Research on adult development and romantic relationships has not yet been undertaken with a lesbian life cycle as the norm. For example, courtship has been rooted in the developmental phase of young heterosexual adulthood by most relationship researchers and developmental psychologists. Most lesbians do not follow this model. Thus, only a few tentative predictions concerning courtship and age were advanced. Specifically, midlife lesbians were expected to be less bound by gender roles, to be more mature in terms of how they approached courtship, as expressed in terms of having more realistic expectations and being aware of their own needs, and to be more skilled at communicating or interpreting interpersonal attraction.

The four significant results reported earlier provide support for the general direction of our predictions; that is, midlife lesbians undertake courtship with greater freedom from gender roles and with more maturity. Midlife lesbians were found to differ significantly from young adults in terms of having been a lesbian longer, perceiving lesbian dating as having the serious goal of commitment, describing lesbian relationships as developing at a rapid pace, and to be more likely to ask for a date and to initiate physical intimacy. Based on our review of each transcript as a whole, we labeled the midlife lesbians as being more "purposive" in their attitudes and behaviors than the young adult or adult group. Midlife lesbians often spoke specifically to the issue of having approached relationships more casually in their youth or having been motivated by physical attraction, sexual gratification, or other needs unrelated to what they considered now to be more important. As they aged, they became more concerned about the "attachment-worthiness" of a partner; that is, whether the necessary warmth, respect, and reciprocal liking necessary to sustain a relationship was present before pursuing a sexual relationship. Once they judged these attributes to be present, they acted quickly. Thus, their current behaviors seemed to be motivated by a more accurate assessment of their needs and greater experience concerning what will sustain a relationship.

Midlife lesbians also spoke to other changes over the course of their lifetime that affected courtship. Many mentioned enjoying no longer having to conform to the butch-femme roles that dominated the bar scene in their youth. They also appreciated the relatively greater freedom they felt to be openly lesbian and being able to find partners outside the bars due to the growth of the lesbian community.

CONCLUSIONS

Courtship was found to be highly relevant to lesbians throughout the life span. Most had established several long-term relationships and utilized a variety of courtship scripts. The friendship and romance scripts were most preferred, with the sexually explicit script having been widely practiced but not preferred. These results suggest that lesbians prefer courtship and relationships that emphasize emotional intimacy either more so or equally with sexual desire, as opposed to favoring sexual attraction over intimacy. Both increasing intimacy and sexuality were used to mark when a relationship was "going beyond" friendship. Contrary to the stereotype of lesbians as being passive in approaching partners, most were found to be quite direct in their verbal expressions of affection, as well as very skilled in the use of proceptive nonverbal cues to signal attraction.

Definitions of lesbian dating and uniqueness, as well as the findings concerning gender roles, illustrated that lesbians either rejected or modified contemporary heterosexual practices. Freedom from gender roles contributed to an egalitarian approach to dating that may have enhanced the intimacy and rapid pacing regarded as unique to lesbian courtship. Most lesbians did not adopt active versus reactive roles in dating. However, those who did rejected heterosexual notions of the woman as the sexual limit-setter. Age and lesbian dating experience also were found to be related to initiating sexual intimacy.

These findings imply that even when lesbians conform to some aspects of heterosexual roles, they do not necessarily reproduce heterosexual power relations in terms of sexual behavior. Furthermore, their courtships may be more sexually satisfying, because satisfaction with sex has been shown to be linked to equality in initiating and refusing sex (Blumstein & Schwartz, 1983).

Courtship among older lesbians was found to differ from younger ones as a function of both maturity and historical change, with midlife lesbians being more oriented toward establishing an emotional commitment, being less tied to gender roles, and expressing appreciation for greater societal tolerance of lesbians. However, conclusions concerning adult development were limited by the small sample size and narrow scope of questions investigated. In addition, the relatively few age differences that were observed suggest that courtship is a strong script in the sense that it is highly codified by cultural norms and may not change much with age. Nevertheless, the results suggest that one interesting area for future research might focus specifically on retrospective evaluations of how courtship has changed over the life course.

Clinical Implications

The findings from the present study have implications for therapists who have lesbian clients. Understanding oneself in relation to others is central to the therapeutic process. Information regarding how lesbians from different age groups negotiate dating and courtship can facilitate this process for clients. Although our sample was limited in size, certain guidelines for therapists can be derived from the data which are consistent with five of the tenets of a feminist theory of psychological practice (Brabeck & Brown, 1997).

Remaining close to the "data of experience." Any theory of lesbian relationship development must remain close to lesbians' real-life experiences–it should be "sappho-centric." Throughout the interview process, participants discussed their relationship histories with candor. We sought meaning of their stories within the context of the relationships we developed with them, and it was our hope to give an accurate voice to their stories. We acknowledge, however, that neither their nor our understanding of relationships is static. Given a different setting or point in time, participants' stories may have varied, and we may have drawn different conclusions. We hope that therapists reading this article will learn as much from the process of our research as they do from the content, and create understanding from both the "data of experience," as well as from human connection.

Embracing diversity. Historically, little has been written about lesbians across the life span. The present research was intended to begin to close this gap in knowledge. Although the participants we interviewed were homogeneous in terms of race and class, their life experiences were quite diverse. It is likely that even more diverse stories may have been obtained using a sample that was more heterogeneous in terms of race, ethnicity, class or ability. We caution therapists to be mindful of the differences among lesbians and to embrace diversity as a foundation for their practice.

Expanding notions of identity and multiple subjectivities. Throughout the research process, we viewed the women as active participants in defining their realities. The interview process was interactive, and at no point did we view ourselves as the only or most important voice of knowledge. During the interviews, we witnessed participants derive new meanings from their relationships and give voice to experiences that previously had been unspoken. Throughout the process, we learned as much about ourselves as we did about participants. For example, based on female socialization, we anticipated that only a minority of lesbians would have participated in casual sexual encounters. Instead, we found that many women had engaged in this script, as well as reported as having learned a great deal about themselves in the process, whereas others rejected the casual sex script entirely. Thus, we recommend that clinicians acknowledge multiple subjectivities within the context of the therapeutic relationship.

Reformulating understanding psychological distress from feminist theory. Traditional psychology places the experiences of the dominant group (e.g., men, heterosexuals) at the center as "normal," "right," or "healthy." The functioning of marginalized groups (e.g., lesbians) is viewed as being deficient by comparison. In terms of relationship development specifically, contemporary heterosexual norms endorse lifelong monogamy as superior to other types of romantic pairings. If the dominant view of permanent pairings as being "better" is internalized by a lesbian client, it may be helpful for the therapist to help her explore alternative paradigms for assessing her own behavior that are based more on lesbian experience. This reformulation takes what was formerly considered to be evidence of a deficit or defect and reinterprets it as evidence of creative resistance in the face of oppression (Brabeck & Brown, 1997).

In conclusion, the findings of the current study can inform therapists' work with lesbian clients. It is our hope that therapists will benefit from both the content and process of the research presented here and will use it to foster growth in their clients.

REFERENCES

Bailey, B. L. (1998). *From front porch to back seat: Courtship in twentieth century America.* Baltimore: The Johns Hopkins University Press.
Bechdel, A. (1997). *Unnatural dykes to watch out for.* Ithaca, NY: Firebrand Books.
Blumstein, P. W., & Schwartz, P. (1983). *American couples.* New York: William Morrow.

Brabeck, M., & Brown, L. (1997). Feminist theory and psychological practice. In J. Worell & N. G. Johnson (Eds.), *Shaping the future of feminist psychology: Education, research, and practice* (pp. 15-35). American Psychological Association: Washington, DC.

Bradford, J., & Ryan, C. (1991). Who we are: Health concerns of middle-aged lesbians. In B. Sang, J. Warshow, & A. Smith (Eds.), *Lesbians at midlife: The creative transition* (pp. 147-163). San Francisco: Spinsters.

Bryant, S., & Demian (1990, May/June). *Partners: Newsletter for gay and lesbian couples* (available from Partners, Box 9685, Seattle, WA 98109).

Cate, R. M., & Lloyd, S. A. (1992). *Courtship*. Newbury Park, CA: Sage.

Cini, M. A., & Malafi, T. N. (1991, March). Paths to intimacy: Lesbian and heterosexual women's scripts of early relationship development. Paper presented at the Association for Women in Psychology conference, Hartford, CT.

DeLaria, L. (1995). Ms. DeLaria's dating tips for dykes. In C. Flowers (Ed.), *Out, loud, and laughing* (pp. 57-68). New York: Anchor.

Eisenbach, H. (1996). *Lesbianism made easy*. New York: Crown.

Gagnon, J. (1977). *Human sexualities*. Glenview, IL: Scott, Foresman.

Ginsberg, G. P. (1988). Rules, scripts and prototypes in personal relationship. In S. W. Duck (Ed.), *Handbook of personal relationships* (pp. 23-39). New York: John Wiley.

Grammick, J. (1984). Developing a lesbian identity. In T. Darty & S. Potter (Eds.), *Women identified women* (pp. 31-44). Palo Alto, CA: Mayfield.

Hall, M., & Gregory, A. (1991). Subtle balances: Love and work in lesbian relationships. In B. Sang, J. Warshow, & A. Smith (Eds.), *Lesbians at midlife: The creative transition* (pp. 122-133). San Francisco: Spinsters.

Kimmel, D. C., & Sang, B. E. (1995). Lesbians and gay men in midlife. In A. R. D'Augelli & C. J. Patterson (Eds.), *Lesbian, gay, and bisexual identities over the life span* (pp. 190-214). New York: Oxford University Press.

Klinkenberg, D., & Rose, S. (1994). Dating scripts of lesbians and gay men. *Journal of Homosexuality, 26,* 23-35.

Lapidus, J. (1995). Procrasti-dating. In K. Jay (Ed.), *Dyke life*. New York: Basic Books.

Laws, J. L., & Schwartz, P. (1977). *Sexual scripts: The social construction of female sexuality*. Washington, DC: University Press of America.

McDaniel, J. (1995). *The lesbian couple's guide*. New York: HarperCollins.

Modell, J. (1983). Dating becomes the way of American youth. In D. Levine, L. P. Moch, L. A. Tilly, J. Modell, & E. Pleck (Eds.), *Essays on the family and historical change* (pp. 169-175). College Station: Texas A & M University Press.

Moore, M. M. (1985). Nonverbal courtship patterns in women: Context and consequences. *Ethology and Sociobiology, 6,* 237-247.

Murstein, B. I. (1974). *Love, sex and marriage through the ages*. New York: Springer.

Peplau, L.A., Rubin, Z., & Hill, C.T. (1977). Sexual intimacy in dating couples. *Journal of Social Issues, 33* (2), 86-109.

Perper, T., & Weis, D. L. (1987). Proceptive and rejective strategies of U.S. and Canadian college women. *Journal of Sex Research, 23,* 455-480.

Rose, S. (1996). Lesbian and gay love scripts. In E. D. Rothblum & L. A. Bond (Eds.), *Preventing heterosexism and homophobia* (pp. 151-173). Newbury Park, CA: Sage.

Rose, S., & Frieze, I. H. (1989). Young singles' contemporary dating scripts. *Sex Roles, 28,* 1-11.

Rose, S., & Frieze, I. H. (1993). Young singles' scripts for a first date. *Gender and Society, 3,* 258-268.

Rose, S., & Roades, L. (1987). Feminism and women's friendships. *Psychology of Women Quarterly, 11,* 243-354.

Rose, S., Zand, D., & Cini, M. (1993). Lesbian courtship scripts. In E. D. Rothblum & K. A. Brehony (Eds.), *Boston marriages: Romantic but asexual relationships among contemporary lesbians* (pp. 70-85). Amherst: University of Massachusetts Press.

Rothblum, E. D., & Brehony, K. A. (1993). *Boston marriages: Romantic but asexual relationships among contemporary lesbians.* Amherst: University of Massachusetts Press.

Sang, B. (1991). Moving towards balance and integration. In B. Sang, J. Warshow, & A. Smith (Eds.), *Lesbians at midlife: The creative transition* (pp. 206-214). San Francisco: Spinsters.

Sausser, G. (1990). *More lesbian etiquette.* Freedom, CA: Crossing Press.

Savin-Williams, R. C. (1995). Dating and romantic relationships among gay, lesbian, and bisexual youths. In R. C. Savin-Williams and K. M. Cohen (Eds.), *The lives of lesbians, gays and bisexuals: Children to adults* (pp. 166-180). New York: Harcourt Brace.

West, C. (1996). *Lesbian polyfidelity.* San Francisco: Bootlegger Publishing.

Beyond "Lesbian Bed Death": The Passion and Play in Lesbian Relationships

Suzanne Iasenza

SUMMARY. Myths about lesbian sexuality continue to exist but none have received such widespread discussion as "lesbian bed death," a myth that has become a clinical entity even though it lacks definitional clarity and empirical validity. Its users, often relying on gender socialization theory, overgeneralize and essentialize lesbian women's sexual experiences, obscuring the diversity of lesbian sexual experience. This paper critiques the use of the term "lesbian bed death" and provides examples from sex research and lesbian literature of the panoply of lesbian passions and play. *[Article copies available for a fee from The Haworth Document Delivery Service: 1-800-HAWORTH. E-mail address: <getinfo@haworthpressinc.com> Website: <http://www.HaworthPress.com> © 2002 by The Haworth Press, Inc. All rights reserved.]*

KEYWORDS. Lesbian, couples, relationships, sexuality, sexual behavior

---

Suzanne Iasenza, PhD, is Associate Professor of Counseling at John Jay College-City University of New York. She is a psychologist and sex therapist in private practice, and is co-editor of the book *Lesbians and psychoanalysis: Revolutions in theory and practice* (Free Press). She is also contributing editor to *In the Family: The Magazine for Lesbians, Gays, Bisexuals, and Their Relations*.

Address correspondence to: Suzanne Iasenza, Counseling Department, John Jay College, CUNY, 445 West 59th St., New York, NY 10019 (E-mail: siasenza@aol.com).

[Haworth co-indexing entry note]: "Beyond 'Lesbian Bed Death': The Passion and Play in Lesbian Relationships." Iasenza, Suzanne. Co-published simultaneously in *Journal of Lesbian Studies* (Harrington Park Press, an imprint of The Haworth Press, Inc.) Vol. 6, No. 1, 2002, pp. 111-120; and: *Lesbian Love and Relationships* (ed: Suzanna M. Rose) Harrington Park Press, an imprint of The Haworth Press, Inc., 2002, pp. 111-120. Single or multiple copies of this article are available for a fee from The Haworth Document Delivery Service [1-800-HAWORTH, 9:00 a.m. - 5:00 p.m. (EST). E-mail address: getinfo@haworthpressinc.com].

111

Given all of the myths about lesbian sexuality it's amazing that any lesbian couple carves out a satisfying sex life. In popular culture lesbian women are often depicted either as the sexually aggressive woman of heterosexual male porno fantasies or as the asexual woman of the Jane Hathaway variety (remember the Beverly Hillbillies?). Lesbian sexual myths involve complex social and political underpinnings and are often confusing. Here are some of the most common: lesbian sex is always satisfying and orgasmic (who better to please a woman than another woman?), lesbian sex occurs constantly (lesbians, like gay men, are obsessed with sex), lesbian sex occurs infrequently (lesbians, like all women, are not socialized to enjoy or want sex), lesbian sex includes mostly hugging and kissing, lesbians only have sex with partners they love, lesbians value emotional closeness over sex, when lesbians "do it" one plays the man (the dominant role) while the other plays the woman (the submissive role), and lesbians are monogamous.

Many elements of these myths are contained within the Grandmommy of all lesbian sex myths, namely, the myth of "Lesbian Bed Death." Defined as a notorious drop-off in sexual activity about two years into long-term lesbian relationships, lesbian bed death, as a concept, has become not only the subject of jokes by lesbian comics but a syndrome that a fair number of lesbian psychotherapy clients and their therapists believe actually exists. As a sex therapist and researcher, I must admit my alarm at the acceptance of a clinical entity whose definitional clarity and empirical validity are at best highly questionable.

A major problem with the use of the term "lesbian bed death," besides its obvious pejorative tone, is that it overgeneralizes and essentializes lesbian women's sexual experiences, obscuring the passion and play of lesbian sexual relating that is shaped by so many factors, besides gender, including the intrapsychic, familial, and interpersonal, as well as race, ethnicity, class, age, able-bodiedness, religion, the coming out process, and political stance. Both sex research literature and writings by lesbian women themselves provide a panoply of lesbian passions. This paper critiques the myth of "lesbian bed death" and uses sex research literature and accounts by lesbian women to provide examples of lesbian passionate play.

A NARROW USE OF SEX RESEARCH

Even before the term "lesbian bed death" was publicly uttered for the first time at a political rally in 1987 (Hyde, 1999), some of the most influential and widely read writers on lesbian sexuality discussed the problems of inhibited sexual desire or infrequency of sexual activity in lesbian relationships (Hall,

1984; Loulan, 1984; Nichols, 1987). These writers relied on the then recent findings of a major research study published in 1983 in a book called *American Couples* by Phillip Blumstein and Pepper Schwartz to support their claims of diminished sexual activity in lesbian women. Blumstein and Schwartz found that lesbian couples indeed had less sex than any other couple—heterosexual married, heterosexual co-habitating or gay male, based on answers to one question: "About how often during the last year have you and your partner had sexual relations?"

Despite the existence of a number of other studies that provided evidence to the contrary (Bressler & Lavender, 1986; Coleman, Hoon & Hoon, 1983; Hedblom, 1973; Jay & Young, 1979; Masters & Johnson, 1979), many writers on women and lesbians over the past fifteen years, many who cite Hall, Loulan, and Nichols's work, also utilize the Blumstein and Schwartz data as the compelling empirical evidence that lesbian relationships suffer from infrequent sexual activity (Carl, 1990; Clunis & Green, 1988; Falco, 1991; MacDonald, 1998). Some even use the term "lesbian bed death" (Angier, 1999; Ogden, 1994; Schwartz, 1998).

The use of the term "lesbian bed death" along with the underlying belief that lesbians, in fact, do have "less sex" than other couples, is problematic both conceptually and empirically. Professional and lay-people alike that use the term are unknowingly conflating two related but separate concepts, sexual infrequency and inhibited sexual desire, whose etiology and development may differ. We do ourselves a grave disservice in relying on a simple sound bite of a term to describe what often involves complex processes. Many lesbian couples who are experiencing sexual desire difficulties, infrequent or unfulfilling sex, like many heterosexual and gay couples, are attempting to manage challenging life issues such as accepting differences in sexuality (activities, desire, and styles) over time, work pressures, trying to have and/or raise children, health issues in themselves or significant others, the impact of menopause, the emotional and physical effects of medications, aging issues, deaths, and the often devastating impact of incest, physical abuse, or sexual assault.

The reliance on the results of one study to provide evidence that lesbian women are less sexual than other couples is a questionable use of research. Many studies have found lesbian women to be more sexually arousable (Coleman et al., 1983; Iasenza, 1991), more sexually assertive (Iasenza, 1991; Masters & Johnson, 1979), and more comfortable using erotic language with a partner (Wells, 1990) than are heterosexual women. Lesbians generally report low levels of orgasmic dysfunction (Coleman et al., 1983; Hedblom, 1973; Jay & Young, 1979; Kinsey, Pomeroy, Martin & Gebhard, 1953) and higher levels of satisfaction with the quality of their sexual lives than do heterosexual women (Bressler & Lavender, 1986; Coleman et al., 1983; Iasenza, 1991; Jay & Young, 1979).

BEYOND A MALE-DEFINED SEXUALITY

The question "how many times" one has sex is one that is based on a male-defined notion of sex, one that, with a penis involved, measures sex in discrete genital acts. Blumstein and Schwartz themselves, in discussing their research, emphasized the importance of integrating non-genital activity when conceptualizing sexuality. Despite their caveat, this type of mechanistic research question is still commonplace even though it neglects the subjective dimension of sex that is an essential part of women's sexual experiences (Tiefer, 1995; Vance, 1983). Lesbian feminist scholar Marilyn Frye (1992), in critiquing such research questions, states, "what 85% of long-term, married couples do more than once a month takes on average 8 minutes to do . . . what we (lesbians) do that, on average, we do considerably less frequently, takes, on average, considerably more than 8 minutes to do. Maybe about 30 minutes at least. Sometimes maybe about an hour" (p. 110).

Masters and Johnson's (1979) study found heterosexual couples to be more focused on genital contact and orgasm than lesbian couples, who integrated more of a whole body experience (kissing, hugging, touching, holding) before including breast or genital contact. They wrote that in heterosexual couples "rarely more than 30 seconds to a minute were spent holding close or caressing the total body area before the breasts or genitals were directly stimulated" (p. 66). Blumstein and Schwartz (1983) noted that in addition to the time taken with whole-body stimulation, lesbian more than heterosexual couples valued reciprocity in the giving and receiving of pleasure. If sex researchers looked more at the time taken to have sex and the variety and reciprocity of sexual activities rather than "how many times" people "have sex," lesbian couples definitely would win the longevity and creativity contests!

Jay and Young's *Gay Report: Lesbians and Gay Men Speak Out About Sexual Experiences and Lifestyles* (1979) further documents the pleasures and passions of lesbian sexual relating. Like Bell and Weinberg (1978) and Blumstein and Schwartz (1983), Jay and Young note no difference in the stated importance of sex between lesbian women and gay men. Unlike Blumstein and Schwartz, they found no difference in sexual frequency between lesbian women and gay men. Most of the lesbian women were satisfied with their sex lives and, like Masters and Johnson (1979) and Loulan (1987), they found that lesbian women enjoyed a variety of ways of pleasuring themselves and their partners, including manual stimulation, tribadism, cunnilingus, kissing, holding, fantasy, and breast play. Most striking was their finding of the generally positive feelings women expressed about their genitals, believed by the authors to be a by-product of the feminist movement. Rather than sexual infrequency, the number one sexual problem Jay and Young's sample identified was lack of communication. Among the many factors that may affect the expression of sexual/affectional feelings, homophobia is often listed as a primary one for many lesbian women. Loulan (1987) reported that the frequency of holding hands changed from 80% of lesbians to 27% in her study when she added the words "in public," a painful example of sexual shame (Rose, 1994).

Sexual variability was the primary characteristic found within samples of lesbian women (and gay men) in Bell and Weinberg's important 1978 study on homosexuality, entitled *Homosexualities: A Study of Diversity Among Men and Women*. Perhaps the most important aspect of their study was the inclusion of comparable samples of black and white lesbians and gay males. Few differences were found between black and white women, including both sexual frequency and general preferences of sexual activities, though black lesbians reported more extensive repertoires than did white lesbians. Age was found to be the primary factor in determining sexual frequency and sexual experimentation. Increase in age was related to lower levels of each. The results of the Jay and Young, Bell and Weinberg, and Joann Loulan studies, combined with those of Blumstein and Schwartz, provide a richer and more complex picture of lesbian sexuality than does the Blumstein and Schwartz data alone.

THE FLEXIBILITY OF SEXUAL SCRIPTS

Many who believe in "lesbian bed death" over-rely on gender socialization theory that posits the idea that a relationship containing two women who have been socialized to be sexually inhibited bodes poorly for the continued sexual vitality of a relationship. Perhaps because I have worked with many heterosexual, gay, and lesbian couples over the years, I don't believe that lesbian couples corner the market on problems with sexual desire, sexual frequency, or in initiating sex. Blumstein and Schwartz found that most couples (lesbian, gay and heterosexual) considered reduced sexual frequency to be a normal part of long-term relating, most likely due to the effects of aging and relationship duration. Come to think of it, I've treated plenty of heterosexual and gay couples who suffer from "lesbian bed death"!

Despite the profound influence sexual scripts exert on people, not all women respond to female socialization in the same way (Laws & Schwartz, 1977; Richardson, 1992). Even Schreurs (1993), in her article on the importance of gender in lesbian sexuality, cites the research "exceptions." Pat Califia's (1979) study is a notable example, in which some lesbian women enjoy recreational sex and prefer nonmonogamy, behaviors that traditionally have been thought to be male behaviors. Assuming that gender is the only or central organizer of sexuality overgeneralizes women's experiences and denies variations in sexual scripts that may be influenced by race, ethnicity, class, and religion, to name a few, or by particular relationship or subcultural contexts. Postmodern thinking (Butler, 1990), emphasizing the fluidity of gender-role and gender subjectivities among and within people, forces us to question the use of a unitary gender socialization theory and renders gender-based concepts like "lesbian bed death" obsolete.

LESBIANS SPEAK OF PASSION AND PLAY

Sex research literature gives us a picture of a diverse and active lesbian sexuality that defies most of our myths. Lesbian sexuality, as briefly described here by lesbian women themselves, also involves a great diversity of turn-ons and passions, many of which illustrate a unique sexual scripting that deconstructs sex/gender dichotomies (activity/passivity, femininity/masculinity, penetrating/being penetrated) and recombines aspects of each, presenting us with examples of fluidity of sexual identifications and desires.

Beverly Burch (1993) offers descriptions of "gender devices and desires" that lesbian partners may use to play with real or imagined gendered sexual selves. One couple she interviewed stated:

Miriam: I love it when she's "femmed up." It's a real sexual turn-on.

Ellen: Miriam would really like us both out in public in heels and nylons.

Miriam: It's the idea of being physical with somebody who's really dressed like a woman. Then this is really lesbian! This is two women! I mean pantyhose and everything! It's a real turn-on to me. The idea of being in a restaurant and sliding my hand under her skirt and over her silky pantyhose. Wow! (p. 117)

In this passionate moment, sameness is the basis of sexual turn-on and femininity is associated with sexual activity in the sliding of a desiring hand under a skirt. The following is an experience of a femme whose receptivity to the touch of her (female) butch lover represents an active passion play in which complementarity is the turn-on:

I begin to imagine myself being *the woman that a woman always wanted.* That's when I begin to eroticize. That's what I begin to feel from my lover's hands . . . I don't want her not to be female to me. Her need is female, but it's butch because I am asking her to expose her desire through the movement of her hands on my body and I'll respond. I want to give up power in response to her need. This can feel profoundly powerful and very unpassive. (Hollibaugh & Moraga, 1983, pp. 398-399; emphasis theirs)

Some lesbian women's passions involve a variety of sexual roles that play out in a versatility and reciprocity in sexual activity. Who best to provide examples of this than Joan Nestle (1998):

I find her under the gown and raise her legs up over my shoulders. My fingers find her open and I push into her, watching her face all the time, the heaving of her breasts. I am fully clothed but naked in my want, in my imagination, in my need to be her lover . . . I grasp the cock I have chosen, the biggest, the longest one that will give her the most pleasure . . . I enter her with it . . . my body behind each thrust . . . Later I play old whore to her younger girl. I will wear my black slip and stockings . . . she will plead for the right to touch me, and then my own fem need will come flooding back . . . and all her perfume will be part of her strength as she enters me with her long fingers dipped in red, not riding me but pushing me to let go. (p. 148-9)

And Dorothy Allison (1994):

So I do like tough women, butch women, big, confident, strong women. I like to twist and turn and roll my fingers down my lover's hips, pull her open vulva to my mouth and work at it, the art and act of pleasuring her. And when she turns to me, I like to scream when I feel the burning heat of her skin on mine. It is then that every part of me opens and sound naturally happens, the sounds not of passion but of joy. Satisfaction. Determined grown-up satisfaction that denies silence, all silences, most particularly the long silence of my childhood, the denial of the lesbian girlchild who was never meant to survive. (p. 152)

These passion plays are examples of lesbian sexuality that shatter old myths, assumptions, and generalizations, like those associated with "lesbian bed death." These lesbian women are not conforming to a single female sexual script. They resist the forces that attempt to inhibit sexual agency and entitlement. As Allison reminds us, lesbian oppression exists and flourishes even now. But these examples represent types of sexual survival and creativity that often get lost in psychological discussions of lesbian sexuality.

How do lesbian women sexually thrive when we were "never meant to survive"? How do we transform "the denial of the lesbian girlchild" into experiences of passion and play? Some clues to these questions reside in the sex research literature where many lesbian women reveal a whole body-whole person sexuality, one that encompasses the use of a variety of sensual/sexual activities, physical sensations, emotional meanings, interpersonal pleasurings and satisfactions. Perhaps we attempt to create a whole from the many fractured parts that result from living within a culture that marks one's sexuality as dangerous, unhealthy, and sinful (Iasenza, 1995).

Other clues spring from our own words and experiences: Audre Lorde's (1984) eloquent use of the erotic as power in everyday life activities or Joan Nestle's (1998) persistent desires whose expression find their roots in working class culture. How do each of us find and maintain connections to our body-psyches? Perhaps it's within a therapy office, or at the local sex club, on the picket line, or between the lines of an Adrienne Rich or Gloria Anzaldua poem. However it happens, we have many examples of resistance and celebration in all of the ways women love women.

At a recent workshop on debunking the "lesbian bed death" term, I asked the participants to explain to me why some lesbian women feel they need such a term. One woman said, "I think talking about it is our way of saying that we deserve the best of everything, including the best sexual lives that are possible." It was helpful for me to hear it put in such a positive frame. And later I thought of other reasons. It gives us a chance to end our isolation and silence about our sexual lives. It creates a dialogue, a language, shared jokes, a type of community, even if it is about one of our "problems." Even though it has little conceptual or empirical validity, it fulfills a community need. I hope in the future we persist in finding new ways to create our sexual dialogues and communities, ones that include the passions and play, the triumphs and celebrations as well.

REFERENCES

Allison, D. (1994). *Skin: Talking about sex, class & literature*. Ithaca, New York: Fire-brand Books.

Angier, N. (1999). *Woman: An intimate geography*. Boston: Houghton Mifflin Company.

Bell, A. P., & Weinberg, M. S. (1978). *Homosexualities: A study of diversity among men and women*. New York: Simon & Schuster.

Blumstein, P. W., & Schwartz, P. (1983). *American couples: Money, work and sex*. New York: William Morrow.

Bressler, L. C., & Lavender, A. D. (1986). Sexual fulfillment of heterosexual, bisexual, and homosexual women. In M. Kehoe (Ed.), *Historical, literary, and erotic aspects of lesbianism* (pp. 109-122). New York: Haworth Press.

Burch, B. (1993). *On intimate terms: The psychology of difference in lesbian relationships.* Urbana and Chicago: University of Illinois Press.

Butler, J. (1990). *Gender trouble: Feminism and the subversion of identity.* New York: Routledge.

Califia, P. (1979). Lesbian sexuality. *Journal of Homosexuality, 4*(3), 255-266.

Carl, D. (1990). *Counseling same-sex couples.* New York: W. W. Norton & Company.

Clunis, D. M., & Green, G. D. (1988). *Lesbian couples.* Seattle: Seal Press.

Coleman, E. M., Hoon, P.W., & Hoon, E. F. (1983). Arousability and sexual satisfaction in lesbian and heterosexual women. *The Journal of Sex Research, 19*(1), 58-73.

Falco, K. L. (1991). *Psychotherapy with lesbian clients: Theory into practice.* New York: Brunner/Mazel.

Fyre, M. (1992). *Willful virgin: Essays in feminism.* Freedom, CA: The Crossing Press.

Hall, M. (1984). Lesbians, limerence and long-term relationships. In J. Loulan, *Lesbian Sex* (pp.141-150). Duluth: Spinsters Ink.

Hedblom, J. H. (1973). Dimensions of lesbian sexual experience. *Archives of Sexual Behavior, 2*(4), 329-341.

Hollibaugh, A., & Moraga, C. (1983). What we're rollin' around in bed with: Sexual silences in feminism. In A. Snitow, C. Stansell, & S. Thompson (Eds.), *Powers of desire: The politics of sexuality* (pp. 394-405). New York: Monthly Review Press.

Hyde, S. (September, 1999). *Personal communication.*

Iasenza, S. (1991). The relations among selected aspects of sexual orientation and sexual functioning in females. *Dissertation Abstracts International.* Ann Arbor: University Microfilms International (No. 9134752).

Iasenza, S. (1995). Platonic pleasures and dangerous desires: Psychoanalytic theory, sex research, and lesbian sexuality. In J. M. Glassgold & S. Iasenza (Eds.), *Lesbians and psychoanalysis: Revolutions in theory and practice* (pp. 345-373). New York: Free Press.

Jay, K., & Young, A. (1979). *The gay report: Lesbians and gay men speak out about sexual experiences and lifestyles.* New York: Summit Books.

Kinsey, A. C., Pomeroy, W. B., Martin, C. E., & Gebhard, P. H. (1953). *Sexual behavior in the human female.* Philadelphia: W. B. Saunders.

Laws, J. L., & Schwartz, P. (1977). *Sexual scripts: The social construction of female sexuality.* Hinsdale, Ill: Dryden Press.

Lorde, A. (1984). *Sister outsider.* Freedom, CA: The Crossing Press.

Loulan, J. (1984). *Lesbian sex.* Duluth: Spinsters Ink.

Loulan, J (1987). *Lesbian passion: Loving ourselves and each other.* San Francisco: Spinsters/aunt lute.

MacDonald, B. J. (1998). Issues in therapy with gay and lesbian couples. *Journal of Sex and Marital Therapy, 24,* 165-190.

Masters, W. H., & Johnson, V. E. (1979). *Homosexuality in perspective.* Massachusetts: Little, Brown & Company.

Nestle, J. (1998). *A fragile union.* CA: Cleis Press.

Nichols, M. (1987). Lesbian sexuality: Issues and developing theory. In Boston Lesbian Psychologies Collective (Ed.), *Lesbian psychologies: Explorations and challenges* (pp. 97-125). Chicago: University of Illinois Press.

Ogden, G. (1994). *Women who love sex.* New York: Pocket Books.

Richardson, D. (1992). Constructing lesbian sexualities: In K. Plummer (Ed.), *Modern homosexualities: Fragments of lesbian and gay experience* (pp. 187-199). London: Routledge.

Rose, S. (1994). Sexual pride and shame in lesbians. In B. Greene & G. M. Herek (Eds.), *Lesbian and gay psychology: Theory, research, and clinical applications* (pp. 71-83). Thousand Oaks: Sage.

Schreurs, K. M. G. (1993). Sexuality in lesbian couples: The importance of gender. *Annual Review of Sex Research, 4,* 49-66.

Schwartz, A. (1998). *Sexual subjects: Lesbians, gender, and psychoanalysis.* New York: Routledge.

Tiefer, L. (1995). *Sex is not a natural act and other essays.* Boulder: Westview Press.

Vance, C.S. (1983). Gender systems, ideology and sex research. In A. Snitow, C. Stansell, & S. Thompson (Eds.), Powers of desire: The politics of sexuality (pp. 371-384). New York: Monthly Review Press.

Wells, J. W. (1990). The sexual vocabularies of heterosexual and homosexual males and females for communicating erotically with a sexual partner. *Archives of Sexual Behavior, 19*(2), 139-147.

Lesbian Intimate Partner Violence: Prevalence and Dynamics

Carolyn M. West

SUMMARY. Researchers have been investigating partner violence for more than 20 years, yet there is a discernible absence of research on interpersonal violence among lesbian couples. Three aspects of lesbian battering are reviewed here. First, the incidence rates and distinct forms that lesbian battering might assume are discussed. Next, the dynamics and correlates of lesbian abuse are highlighted. The concluding section focuses on suggestions for intervention. *[Article copies available for a fee from The Haworth Document Delivery Service: 1-800-HAWORTH. E-mail address: <getinfo@haworthpressinc.com> Website: <http://www.HaworthPress.com> © 2002 by The Haworth Press, Inc. All rights reserved.]*

KEYWORDS. Lesbian partner violence, battering, domestic violence, same-sex domestic violence, intimate partner violence, interventions

---

Carolyn M. West, PhD, is Assistant Professor of Psychology in the Interdisciplinary Arts & Sciences Program at the University of Washington, Tacoma. Her current research focuses on ethnic minority partner violence and the long-term consequences of child sexual abuse.

Address correspondence to: Carolyn M. West, PhD, Assistant Professor of Psychology, University of Washington, Tacoma, Interdisciplinary Arts & Sciences, Box 358436, 1900 Commerce Street, Tacoma, WA 98402-3100 (www.drcarolynwest.com).

[Haworth co-indexing entry note]: "Lesbian Intimate Partner Violence: Prevalence and Dynamics." West, Carolyn M. Co-published simultaneously in *Journal of Lesbian Studies* (Harrington Park Press, an imprint of The Haworth Press, Inc.) Vol. 6, No. 1, 2002, pp. 121-127; and: *Lesbian Love and Relationships* (ed: Suzanna M. Rose) Harrington Park Press, an imprint of The Haworth Press, Inc., 2002, pp. 121-127. Single or multiple copies of this article are available for a fee from The Haworth Document Delivery Service [1-800-HAWORTH, 9:00 a.m. - 5:00 p.m. (EST). E-mail address: getinfo@haworthpressinc.com].

121

Although researchers have discovered substantial rates of intimate partner violence among both heterosexual and same-sex couples, violence in lesbian relationships is understudied. This oversight has been attributed to discrimination, most notably homophobia, the irrational fear and hatred of lesbians, and heterosexism, or the belief that heterosexuality is normative. Partially due to these forms of discrimination, investigators have developed theories that conceptualize violence as involving male perpetrators and female victims, which contributes to the invisibility of lesbian battering. Moreover, the fear of reinforcing negative stereotypes has led some community members, activists, and victims to deny the extent of violence among lesbians (Renzetti & Miley, 1996). Despite the silence around this topic, literature reviews (Burke & Follingstad, 1999; West, 1998), empirical studies (e.g., Lie, Schilit, Bush, Montagne, & Reyes, 1991; Lockhart, White, Causby, & Isaac, 1994), interviews, clinical observations, and personal stories (Leventhal & Lundy, 1999; Renzetti & Miley, 1996) indicate that interpersonal violence is an alarmingly frequent occurrence among lesbians. Three aspects of lesbian battering are reviewed here. First, the incidence rates and distinct forms that lesbian battering might assume are discussed. Next, the dynamics and correlates of lesbian abuse are highlighted. The concluding section focuses on suggestions for intervention.

RATES OF VICTIMIZATION

It is difficult to obtain accurate estimates of partner violence in lesbian relationships. Researchers have relied on small, self-selected, nonrandom samples, which were often recruited from one geographical location, such as San Francisco, or participants who were contacted through lesbian social and friendship networks. Consequently, White, middle-class, educated lesbians who were open about their sexual orientation were overrepresented in most studies. To date, little is known about other members of the lesbian community, including adolescents, women of color, and bisexual women (Leventhal & Lundy, 1999).

In addition, the literature has been plagued by methodological problems. For example, researchers have used differing time frames (violence in a current relationship vs. any instance of relationship violence). Instruments to measure violence also have differed across studies. Some investigators have used subjective measures of violence, for instance, items such as, "If you are currently in a lesbian relationship, is it abusive?" In contrast, other researchers have used standardized measures, such as the Conflict Tactics Scale. In addition, many researchers have measured the occurrence of violence without determining if the surveyed participant was a victim or aggressor. These limitations make it difficult to interpret findings and to compare rates of violence across studies (for a review of methodological limitations see Burke & Follingstad, 1999).

Despite these research limitations, it is clear that lesbian battering is a serious social concern. The reported rates of physical violence within lesbian relationships vary widely, with estimates ranging from a low of 8.5% to a high of 73% in former lesbian relationships. Most studies found that between 30-40% of surveyed participants had been involved in at least one relationship with a female partner where an incident of physical abuse occurred. Pushing, shoving, and slapping were the most commonly reported forms of abuse, while beatings and assaults with weapons were less frequent. Sexual violence also may be present in lesbian relationships, with estimates ranging from a low of 7% to a high of 55% in previous lesbian relationships. Victims experienced a broad range of types of abuse, including forced kissing, breast and genital fondling, and oral, anal, or vaginal penetration. Victimization rates increased dramatically when psychological and verbal abuse was assessed, with more than 80% of surveyed participants reporting this form of abuse. Common forms included threats and verbal abuse, such as being called names, yelled at, and insulted (for reviews see Burke & Follingstad, 1999; Waldner-Haugrud, 1999; West, 1998).

The rates and types of abuse experienced by battered lesbians are comparable to those reported by their heterosexual counterparts. Furthermore, the pattern of abuse is similar across sexual orientation. More specifically, the limited research suggests that lesbian battering tends to increase in severity and frequency over the course of the abusive relationship (Renzetti, 1998).

However, there are several important differences between violence in lesbian and heterosexual relationships. A lesbian batterer can use homophobic control as a method of psychological abuse, which further isolates the victim. For example, an abuser may "out" her partner without permission by revealing her sexual orientation to others, including relatives, employers, and landlords, and in child custody cases. This form of abuse could result in a variety of negative consequences for the victim, such as being shunned by family members and the loss of children, a job and housing (Renzetti, 1998).

Another significant difference is that lesbians must contend with additional myths surrounding their partner violence. The role of the victim or aggressor cannot be determined based on gender in same-sex relationships. Consequently, researchers and members of law enforcement may falsely believe that violence is enacted by the partner who is more "masculine" in appearance or demeanor, while the victim possesses more "feminine" characteristics. The research dispels this myth. Lesbians do not generally mimic heterosexual roles, and lesbian batterers are not consistently more masculine than their victims in terms of physical size, appearance, or mannerism (Renzetti, 1998).

Lesbian victims also must contend with the myth of mutual battering. Lesbian battering is seldom reciprocal violence; rather, it involves a primary aggressor and victim. Like their heterosexual counterparts, a lesbian victim may be quiet, withdrawn, and embarrassed, particularly if she has defended herself or fought back. Although she may blame herself, further questioning reveals that what appears to be "mutual abuse" is actually the victim's efforts to secure her personal safety, as opposed to hurting her partner. In addition, she may express concern for her partner's well-being and often continue to assume responsibility for the violence long after the relationship has ended. In contrast, batterers often loudly assert their victimization status, while simultaneously displaying controlling and intrusive behavior. They rarely express shame or even remorse. Although they may perceive themselves as partially accountable for the relationship violence, they seldom accept full responsibility. Instead, they blame the victim for provoking the violence (Leventhal & Lundy, 1999; Renzetti & Miley, 1996).

DYNAMICS OF LESBIAN BATTERING

Researchers have investigated various dynamics and correlates of same-sex partner violence. Some investigators have focused on risk factors that are unique to lesbians. For example, researchers argue that societal discrimination fosters homophobia, which becomes internalized when lesbians accept society's negative evaluations of them and incorporates these beliefs into their self-concept. This in turn may contribute to low self-esteem, feelings of powerlessness, denial of group membership, and difficulty establishing committed, trusting relationships. These negative feelings are then acted out in the form of lesbian battering. Although plausible, this theory awaits further empirical investigation. Other researchers have investigated the association between the intergenerational transmission of abuse, for example, witnessing or experiencing violence in the family of origin, and substance abuse, relationship dependency, and power imbalances. Although all these factors can be related to abuse across sexual orientation, there are some important differences for lesbian couples (Burke & Follingstad, 1999; Renzetti, 1998; West, 1998), which will be discussed below.

Regardless of sexual orientation, there is a complex association between intergenerational transmission of violence and adult involvement in intimate partner abuse. The difference is that lesbians may be at increased risk for verbal and physical abuse by family members when they reveal their sexual orientation (Leventhal & Lundy, 1999). Although some researchers failed to link lesbian battering to violence in the family of origin, other investigators found an association between victimization and/or perpetration of violence in a current or past lesbian relationship and a history of child abuse or witnessing parental aggression (Lie et al., 1991).

The association between substance abuse and partner violence is also complicated. Alcohol use can facilitate and legitimate intimate violence; however, the general consensus among family violence researchers is that alcohol consumption does not cause the abuse. This is true for lesbian relationships as well. In fact, some researchers found no association between lesbian battering and alcohol/substance abuse (Renzetti, 1998; West, 1998). However, the centrality of bars in the social lives of some lesbians, coupled with societal discrimination that fosters alienation and isolation, may contribute to both heavy drinking and partner violence. Not surprisingly, other researchers discovered that the frequency of alcohol use by respondents was correlated with the number of abusive acts that were both perpetrated and sustained in lesbian relationships (Schilit, Lie, & Montagne, 1990).

The path between substance abuse and lesbian battering appears to be mediated by relationship dependency. Researchers speculate that lesbians who feel dependent may use alcohol to feel more assertive and powerful. When inhibitions become loosened, the aggressor may then resort to relationship violence. Equally as important, a correlation was found between a batterer's dependency on her partner and the frequency and severity of abuse inflicted. Alternatively stated, the greater the batterer's dependency and the greater the victim's desire to be independent, the more likely the batterer is to enact more types of aggression with greater frequency (Renzetti, 1998).

Similar dynamics also may exist in violent heterosexual relationships. The difference, however, is that women are socialized to define themselves in relation to significant others and to place a high value on intimacy. Thus, when two women are romantically involved, it may be even more difficult for them to establish a sense of independence and autonomy in their relationship. In addition, the lack of social validation and support may lead lesbians to establish a greater attachment to their partners. Although this sense of intimacy may act as a buffer against discrimination, it also may create a sense of "fusion" or "merging," which can make it difficult for each partner to have a sense of independence and separate identity in the relationship. As a result, having a different opinion or initiating social activities without the partner might be perceived as rejection, which in turn leads to conflict and possibly physical violence (Renzetti, 1998). Empirical studies support this contention. Lockhart and associates (1994) discovered that lesbians who reported severe levels of physical abuse perceived that their partners had a high need for social fusion, as measured by such beliefs as couples need to do everything together. Severely victimized respondents also reported more conflict around issues of independence and autonomy, such as a partner's emotional and financial dependency, a partner socializing without the respondent, and a respondent's intimate involvement with other people.

Conflicts around dependency and autonomy may be exacerbated by power imbalances in the relationship. Although the link between power imbalances and battering is less clear among same-sex couples, it is worthy of consideration. Social class and intellectual differences between lesbian partners have been associated with batterers hitting, choking, and pushing their partners. In addition, lesbian battering has been associated with an imbalance in the division of household labor, such as cooking and managing finances (Burke & Follingstad, 1999; Lockhart et al., 1994).

In conclusion, the research on dynamics and correlates of lesbian battering is limited and often contradictory. Internalized homophobia may be a significant contributor. However, it appears that prior exposure to violence, alcohol use, relationship dependency, and power imbalances can contribute to partner violence across sexual orientation. Nevertheless, it is important to consider how these dynamics differ in violent lesbian relationships.

SUGGESTIONS FOR INTERVENTION

Based on a review of the literature (Leventhal & Lundy, 1999; West, 1998), the following recommendations are made:

1. Identifying the problem is the first step to motivating the lesbian community and service providers to recognize and confront same-sex battering. This entails such actions as broadening the language in partner violence laws to ensure that victims are equally protected regardless of sexual orientation. Defining the problem also involves conducting more empirical research on the prevalence and incidence of same-sex partner violence, characteristics of the violence, and dynamics.
2. Extensive training is needed for service providers in law enforcement, social service agencies, and the medical and mental health professions. Professionals need to address homophobia and discrimination against lesbians in their agencies and to develop written and spoken language that is inclusive of same-sex relationships. This will enable victims to feel more comfortable revealing their sexual orientation and their abuse.
3. Massive intervention efforts should be directed toward the lesbian community. These intervention strategies could include newspaper advertisements, telephone books that specifically list services for same-sex partner violence, and flyers posted at parades and conferences that attract

large gatherings of lesbians. A special effort should be made to reach lesbians of color and adolescents. Services based in the lesbian community, such as shelters and advocacy, need to be expanded and made available outside the few large urban areas in which they currently exist.

4. Finally, factors that contribute to same-sex partner violence must be addressed within the lesbian community and by help providers, including denial of the problem of abuse among lesbians, internalized homophobia, prior exposure to violence, and substance abuse.

CONCLUSION

There is no doubt that intimate partner violence occurs among lesbians. Evidence indicates that it may be as prevalent as among heterosexuals and that a full range of types of violence occurs, including verbal, psychological, physical, and sexual abuse. Some of the dynamics associated with such violence appears to be unique to lesbians due to the social stigma and discrimination they experience. In addition, resources to help lesbian victims are lacking. However, research uncovering the extent of the problem has begun to suggest what interventions might be effective.

REFERENCES

Burke, L. K., & Follingstad, D. R. (1999). Violence in lesbian and gay relationships: Theory, prevalence, and correlational factors. *Clinical Psychology Review, 19*(5), 487-512.

Leventhal, B., & Lundy, S. E. (Eds.). (1999). *Same-sex domestic violence: Strategies for change.* Thousand Oaks, CA: Sage.

Lie, G. Y., Schilit, R., Bush, J., Montagne, M., & Reyes, L. (1991). Lesbians in currently aggressive relationships: How frequently do they report aggressive past relationships? *Violence and Victims, 6*(2), 121-135.

Lockhart, L. L., White, B. W., Causby, V., & Isaac, A. (1994). Letting out the secret: Violence in lesbian relationships. *Journal of Interpersonal Violence, 9*(4), 469-492.

Renzetti, C. M. (1998). Violence and abuse in lesbian relationships: Theoretical and empirical issues. In R. K. Bergen (Ed.), *Issues in intimate violence.* Thousand Oaks, CA: Sage.

Renzetti, C. M., & Miley, C. H. (1996). *Violence in gay and lesbian domestic partnerships.* Binghamton, NY: Harrington Park Press.

Schilit, R., Lie, G. Y., & Montagne, M. (1990). Substance use as a correlate of violence in intimate lesbian relationships. *Journal of Homosexuality, 19*(3), 51-65.

Waldner-Haugrud, L. K. (1999). Sexual coercion in lesbian and gay relationships: A review and critique. *Aggression and Violent Behavior, 4*(2), 139-149.

West, C. M. (1998). Leaving a second closet: Outing partner violence in same-sex couples. In J. L. Jasinski & L. M. Williams (Eds.), *Partner violence: A comprehensive review of 20 years of research* (pp. 163-183). Thousand Oaks, CA: Sage.

Couples Therapy for Lesbians: Understanding Merger and the Impact of Homophobia

Maryka Biaggio
Suz Coan
Wendi Adams

SUMMARY. Lesbian couples are similar to their heterosexual counterparts in many ways, but there are some ways in which lesbian relationships are unique. The focus here is on how couples therapists can be well informed about some key aspects of lesbian couples and their experi-

Maryka Biaggio (PhD, Utah State University, 1977) is Professor and Director of Research on Feminist Issues at the School of Professional Psychology, Pacific University, Forest Grove, Oregon. Her scholarly interests and publications are primarily in the areas of psychology of women and dual relationship ethical issues. She is a past Chair of the Board of the Association for Women in Psychology and a fellow of Division 35 of the American Psychological Association.

Suz Coan (MS, Pacific University, 2002) is a doctoral student at the School of Professional Psychology, Pacific University, Forest Grove, Oregon. Her research interests include diversity issues within lesbian couples therapy, bisexual-lesbian relationships and political aspects of bisexuality.

Wendi Adams (MS, Pacific University, 1999) is a doctoral student at the School of Professional Psychology, Pacific University, Forest Grove, Oregon. Her academic/research interests are in the area of psychology of women and the application of dialectic behavior therapy with various clinical populations. She is a past president of the School of Professional Psychology Student Association.

Address correspondence to: Maryka Biaggio, Professional Psychology, Pacific University, 2004 Pacific Avenue, Forest Grove, OR 97116 (E-mail: biaggiom@pacificu.edu).

[Haworth co-indexing entry note]: "Couples Therapy for Lesbians: Understanding Merger and the Impact of Homophobia." Biaggio, Maryka, Suz Coan, and Wendi Adams. Co-published simultaneously in *Journal of Lesbian Studies* (Harrington Park Press, an imprint of The Haworth Press, Inc.) Vol. 6, No. 1, 2002, pp. 129-138; and: *Lesbian Love and Relationships* (ed: Suzanna M. Rose) Harrington Park Press, an imprint of The Haworth Press, Inc., 2002, pp. 129-138. Single or multiple copies of this article are available for a fee from The Haworth Document Delivery Service [1-800-HAWORTH, 9:00 a.m. - 5:00 p.m. (EST). E-mail address: getinfo@haworthpressinc.com].

129

ences, most notably their experience of homophobia, and the phenomenon of merger in the lesbian relationship. Because of the pervasive nature of homophobia, it is essential that therapists recognize that homophobia impacts lesbians and their relationships in a myriad of ways. Merger has often been viewed as a problem in lesbian relationships, but the emotional intensity of such relationships should not be misunderstood or interpreted as problematic; to do so assumes that heterosexual relationships are the norm and that relationship styles which differ from this norm are somehow aberrant (Burch, 1986). Therapists who understand these aspects of the lesbian relationship are better prepared to provide an affirmative therapy experience to the lesbian couple. *[Article copies available for a fee from The Haworth Document Delivery Service: 1-800-HAWORTH. E-mail address: <getinfo@haworthpressinc.com> Website: <http://www.HaworthPress.com> © 2002 by The Haworth Press, Inc. All rights reserved.]*

KEYWORDS. Lesbian, couples, couples therapy, couples counseling, coming out, merger, homophobia

Lesbian couples are, in many ways, similar to their heterosexual counterparts. All couples, regardless of sexual orientation, must grapple with an array of issues that present themselves over the life of a relationship. They must navigate dating and the "getting to know each other" stage, they must negotiate the inevitable conflicts of an intimate relationship, and they must sometimes deal with the relationship's demise. In these ways lesbian couples resemble heterosexual couples, and research by Kurdek (1994) has demonstrated that the processes that regulate relationship satisfaction are similar across homosexual and heterosexual relationships.

However, there are some ways in which lesbian relationships are unique, and in order for lesbian couples to be well served in therapy, therapists must understand the unique aspects of these relationships (Curtis, 1994). For instance, all lesbians, both as individuals and as members of a couple, are confronted with the pervasive experience of heterosexism and homophobia.

Another important way in which lesbian couples differ from heterosexual and gay male couples is with respect to the level of intimacy in the relationship. This paper will discuss these important aspects of lesbian relationships–intimacy, merger, and the impact of homophobia.

For the most part, the therapy techniques that are utilized for heterosexual couples can be employed with the lesbian couple, as long as there is the usual sensitivity to how the members of the couple will respond to specific interventions. The school of therapy as well as the therapist's sex or sexual orientation may be of some importance in couples therapy, since some lesbian couples may prefer to work with a woman or lesbian therapist. Politically astute lesbians may request a lesbian affirmative or feminist therapist. These issues are important but will not be discussed in this paper since our focus will be on how couples therapists can be well informed about some key aspects of lesbian couples and their experiences.

THE IMPACT OF HOMOPHOBIA ON THE LESBIAN COUPLE

Lesbians, by virtue of their sexual orientation, are confronted with prejudice and discrimination in both obvious and subtle ways. Although some strides have been made in recent years, lesbianism is still not widely accepted within U.S. society. This, of course, has implications for how lesbians feel about and represent themselves and their relationships to their family, friends, and society in general. Some environments, such as feminist communities or liberal urban areas, are fairly accepting of lesbianism. Others, like small rural communities or areas predominated by conservative influences, can be nonaccepting and even hostile. But the boundaries in any given social setting are somewhat fluid; there are always new people flowing into communities. Lesbians thus meet new people on an ongoing basis, and continually grapple with the question of coming out.

The decision to come out is both an individual and relationship decision. Lesbians typically find that they must discriminate among various groups of people; they may be out in their circle of friends, but they may not have revealed the nature of their intimate relationship nor even their sexual orientation to their family. Many lesbians find that their families of origin are disappointed in what is perceived as their failure to have a traditional marriage, and the members of the couple are left feeling that they are on their own as they build their relationship. In fact, Kurdek and Schmitt (1987) found that married couples perceived more support from family members than did gay and lesbian couples.

The decision to come out to any sphere of friends or family is not one that is made lightly, since it can permanently affect important relationships and one's social circle. This decision may not only be difficult for the individual, but the potential for conflict within the lesbian relationship is high. Differences between members of a couple with respect to coming out decisions can lead to conflict in the relationship and difficulties in their social circles. Such differences are full of opportunities for misunderstanding and hurt, since the failure of one person to be as out as the other may be interpreted as shame about that partner or the relationship. Navigating differences in these feelings and making decisions about coming out may be especially challenging in newly formed relationships.

It is also the case that lesbians cannot avail themselves of the benefits of marriage, which offers not only legal and financial advantages but also the stamp of legitimacy. Thus, lesbians' experiences of social acceptance and support are altogether different from those of heterosexuals.

Negative cultural attitudes take a toll on the individual, and internalized homophobia can create difficulties for the lesbian couple, perhaps resulting in a devaluation of their relationship. MacDonald (1998) notes that one of the most common recommendations made in the couples therapy literature dealing with lesbian couples is the normalization of their problems: "Antihomosexual attitudes can lead . . . lesbian partners to blame their problems not on their relationship but on their homosexuality" (p. 186).

It is essential that therapists recognize that heterosexism and homophobia impact lesbians and their relationships in a myriad of ways. According to MacDonald (1998, p. 166): "All of the issues presented by gay and lesbian clients and their resolution in therapy may be influenced by homophobia and the characteristics and biases of the therapist." Thus, the therapist must also confront his/her own biases in order to provide lesbians with an affirmative therapy experience.

INTIMACY AND MERGER IN LESBIAN RELATIONSHIPS

Lesbian couples may differ from other relationship types with respect to equality and intimacy. For instance, there is research indicating that lesbians place more emphasis on and practice equality between partners to a greater extent than is the case for heterosexual relationships. Blumstein and Schwartz (1983), in their study of American couples, noted: "Our data have told us that lesbians hold up, as the ideal relationship, one where two strong women come together in total equality" (p. 310).

Much has been written about women and intimacy, as well as sex differences in intimacy. There is research to support the contention that women in general are more focused on and desirous of emotional intimacy in their social and intimate relationships than are men. For instance, Peplau (1991) has presented evidence that sex is a strong determinant of relationship style. Specifically, Peplau explains that sexual frequency with an intimate partner is greatest among gay men, intermediate among heterosexuals, and lowest among lesbians. Also, sexual exclusivity among couples is least common among gay males, and lesbians differ sharply from gay men in their rates of exclusivity. Zacks, Green, and Marrow (1988) found lesbian relationships to be much more cohesive then heterosexual relationships. Burch (1997) holds that lesbians desire and find a high degree of intimacy in their relationships and also desire and spend more time together than other kinds of partners. Taken together, these data suggest that lesbian relationships are less focused on sexual novelty and frequency and more likely to be cohesive, intimate, and sexually exclusive than other relationship types. This may reflect a high level of interest in commitment, trust, and emotional intimacy between lesbian partners.

A number of writers have noted that lesbian relationships are more likely than other intimate relationships to be characterized by merger (e.g., Burch, 1985; Igartua, 1998; Krestan & Bepko, 1980). Merger, which has also been called fusion and enmeshment, has been described as "a relational process in which the boundaries between the individual partners are blurred and a premium is placed on togetherness and emotional closeness" (Ossana, 2000, p. 281). Although merger is a common experience in lesbian relationships, it is not nonexistent in other relationship types: "Merger does occur between men or opposite sex partners, but frequently not as strongly or pervasively as with women" (Gray & Isensee, 1996, p. 96). Nor is merger evident in all lesbian relationships. For instance, Hill (1999) interviewed members of eight lesbian couples and concluded that fusion did not characterize these lesbian relationships in general. And in a study of 275 lesbians from a nonclinical sample, Causby, Lockhart, White, and Greene (1995) found that the extent of fusion in lesbian relationships was moderate and not excessive as some earlier works have indicated.

Some authors have discussed merger in lesbian relationships as a problem, but others have suggested that the emotional intensity of such relationships should not be misunderstood or interpreted as problematic; to do so assumes that heterosexual relationships are the norm and that relationship styles which differ from this norm are somehow aberrant (Burch, 1986). While merger is often a feature of the lesbian relationship, it may or may not be a part of the presenting complaint for a couple in therapy. As Igartua (1998) explains, lesbians function comfortably at greater levels of merger than heterosexuals. Thus, the therapist should not assume that the presence of merger in a lesbian relationship indicates a problem in relating.

Lesbian relationships are different from heterosexual relationships in some ways, and these relationships should be accepted on their own terms. The high levels of intimacy found in many lesbian relationships may be especially valued and sought out by lesbians! In fact, Burch (1997, pp. 93-94) notes: "The desire for a close emotional connection seems to be the primary mark of lesbian relationships. Attachment, emotional involvement, intimacy, and general closeness are highly correlated with satisfaction in lesbian relationships." And, as Ossana (2000) has pointed out, lesbian couples may merge as a means to strengthen their identity in a culture that largely negates their existence. Understood in this context, merger may not only be desirable for lesbians in relationships, but may also be in part an adaptive response to adverse conditions.

Thus, it is not axiomatic that merger is an indication of concern or dysfunction. We contend that the level of intimacy that is shared by a couple exists on a continuum, with merger situated at one end of the continuum, and a high level of emotional separation at the other end. Whether or not a given couple experiences conflict or difficulties with respect to intimacy issues will be a function of their values, desires, and actual experiences of and satisfaction with intimacy and autonomy in their relationship.

It is the therapist's responsibility at the outset of therapy to assess each partner's perspectives on the nature of the difficulties that have brought the couple to therapy. This requires that the therapist understand the general nature of the lesbian relationship and not impose a heterosexual standard on the couple. How, then, does the therapist respect the unique nature of the lesbian relationship while accurately assessing specific relationships? We propose that the therapist (1) be well informed about lesbian relationships and culture; (2) respect the individuals' reports and views of the nature of their difficulties; and (3) focus on a functional analysis of the relationship.

Being well informed about lesbian relationships and culture requires that the therapist understand the unique nature of these relationships and the sociocultural context in which they operate. It is also important that the therapist not make assumptions about what might constitute problematic relating. For instance, lesbian couples often report high levels of shared activities; the therapist who understands lesbian relationships and respects the clients' reports will not assume that such a report is indicative of a problem. Rather, the therapist should ascertain what the individual members of the relationship consider problematic. This, of course, is indicative of a functional analysis: arriving at an understanding of how the relationship functions and in what ways the actual patterns of relating are creating problems for members of the couple.

If merger is a concern to a lesbian couple, their concern may be expressed in a variety of ways. "Occasionally, one or both partners will name it as the issue by expressing their sense that they are too close; saying, for example that their lives are wrapped up in each other" (Burch, 1986, p. 60). But couples may also note other problems which are indicative of merger: one person withdrawing emotionally and/or sexually, or the couple engaging in frequent struggles over autonomy and closeness. Or couples may express difficulties confronting and addressing conflict: "In merged couples, couple harmony may become the primary issue so that partners deny differences and avoid, rather than resolve, conflict" (Causby et al., 1995, p. 73). Burch (1986) notes that a particular clinical picture is likely to emerge when merger problems are brought to therapy:

> Usually one partner is more overtly unhappy than the other with their enmeshed state. She may express it directly, or she may act out the need for separateness by withdrawing, having an affair, being overly critical, or threatening to leave . . . . The other then takes the role of pursuing the connection between the two of them and reestablishing intimacy. They get stuck in these roles and come to believe that their roles are created by their individual natures; one says she is the type who needs distance, the other says she needs more closeness . . . (F)urther exploration sometimes reveals that they did not take these same roles in previous relationships. They are not simply opposites but have dynamically created their polarity. (p. 61)

When merger is a therapeutic issue, the couple therapist must address three general themes with the couple: (1) understanding and managing the polarization of roles that results from conflict over merger/separation; (2) facilitating an understanding of each other's views about intimacy; and (3) fostering the skills required to negotiate the problems that have resulted from concerns over merger.

By explaining the polarization that typically occurs when merger is an issue, members of the couple come to understand the problem as one *between* them, rather than something for which they may blame *the other*. Burch (1982, pp. 203-204) explains it this way: "Most important, the therapist can talk about the dynamic between lovers in which they disown part of their feelings and allow their partner to act them out for them–that somewhere in themselves is the other side of the polarity they have created. For some couples this cognitive input is both permission and catalyst." This exercise can facilitate work on breaking out of the polarized roles. Helping members of the couple break the pattern of polarized roles can also lead to a discussion about their views and frustrations with respect to intimacy in their relationship, and how to better understand and have empathy for each other's position. "By exploring the similarities and differences between partners' values and expectations, the therapist is acknowledging the fact that there is no standard level of closeness, and is also modeling the kind of comparative exploration that couples must engage in when confronting potentially conflictual issues" (Pardie & Herb, 1997, p. 56). Of course, an important end goal of this whole process is the fostering of skills that will assist the couple in renegotiating their style of relating. The therapist should not only assist the individuals in developing these skills, but also encourage implementation and practice of them: "Conscious relationships and intimacy are dances, and these dance steps can be learned, but must be practiced often to develop a high degree of skill" (Gray & Isensee, 1996, p. 104).

CONCLUSIONS

Unfortunately, misconceptions about lesbian relationships abound. Peplau, Cochran, and Mays (1997) note that stereotypes often depict lesbian relationships as unhappy. This has been borne out in some research in which heterosexual students judged lesbian and gay relationships to be less satisfying, more prone to discord, and less in love then heterosexual couples (Testa, Kinder, & Ironson, 1987). However, there is much research indicating that the quality of relationships is generally similar for lesbian, gay male, and heterosexual couples (e.g., Duffy & Rusbult, 1986; Kurdek, 1994; Kurdek & Schmitt, 1986). It is important that couples therapists working with lesbians examine their attitudes about lesbianism and take responsibility for challenging myths or stereotypes they may hold.

Therapists should be sensitive to the ways in which lesbian couples are unique and should also have an understanding of the ways in which lesbian couples vary. The practice of competent and ethical therapy requires an understanding about the persons a therapist works with and an examination of attitudes that may interfere with good practice. According to Ossana (2000, p. 297): "Therapists who go beyond an attitude of passive acceptance to one of active validation and affirmation provide an invaluable service to their clients." This, indeed, should be the approach that the therapist strives to take with the lesbian couple.

REFERENCES

Blumstein, P., & Schwartz, P. (1983). *American couples: Money, work, sex.* New York: Simon & Schuster.

Burch, B. (1982). Psychological merger in lesbian couples: A joint ego psychological and systems approach. *Family Therapy, 9*(3), 201-208.

Burch, B. (1985). Another perspective on merger in lesbian relationships. In L.B. Rosewater & L. Walker (Eds.), *Handbook of feminist therapy: Women's issues in psychotherapy* (pp. 100-109). New York: Springer.

Burch, B. (1986). Psychotherapy and the dynamics of merger in lesbian couples. In T. Stein & C. Cohen (Eds.), *Contemporary perspectives on psychotherapy with lesbians and gay men* (pp. 57-71). New York: Plenum Publishing.

Burch, B. (1997). *Other women: Lesbian/bisexual experience and psychoanalytic views of women.* New York: Columbia University Press.

Causby, V., Lockhart, L., White, B., & Greene, K. (1995). Fusion and conflict resolution in lesbian relationships. In C. T. Tully (Ed.), *Lesbian social services: Research issues* (pp. 67-82). New York: Harrington Park Press.

Curtis, F. (1994). Gestalt couples therapy with lesbian couples: Applying theory and practice to the lesbian experience. In G. Wheeler & S. Backman (Eds.), *On intimate ground: A gestalt approach to working with couples* (pp. 188-209). San Francisco: Jossey-Bass Publishers.

Duffy, S.M., & Rusbult, C.E. (1986). Satisfaction and commitment in homosexual and heterosexual relationships. *Journal of Homosexuality, 12*, 1-24.

Gray, D., & Isensee, R. (1996). Balancing autonomy and intimacy in lesbian and gay relationships. In C. J. Alexander, PhD (Ed.), *Gay and lesbian mental health: A sourcebook for practitioners* (pp. 95-104). NY: Harrington Park Press.

Hill, C. A. (1999). Fusion and conflict in lesbian relationships? *Feminism & Psychology, 9*(2), 179-185.

Igartua, K. (1998). Therapy with lesbian couples: The issues and the interventions. *Canadian Journal of Psychiatry, 43*, 391-396.

Krestam, J., & Bepko, C.L. (1980). The problem of fusion in the lesbian couple. *Family Process, 19*, 277-289.

Kurdek, L.A. (1994). The nature and correlates of relationship quality in gay, lesbian, and heterosexual cohabiting couples. In B. Greene & G.M. Herek (Eds.), *Lesbian and gay psychology: Theory, research, and clinical applications* (pp. 133-155). Thousand Oaks, CA: Sage Publications.

Kurdek, L.A., & Schmitt, J.P. (1986). Relationship quality of partners in heterosexual married, heterosexual cohabiting, and gay and lesbian relationships. *Journal of Personality and Social Psychology, 51*, 711-720.

Kurdek, L.A., & Schmitt, J.P. (1987). Perceived emotional support from family and friends in members of homosexual, married, and heterosexual cohabiting couples. *Journal of Homosexuality, 14*, 57-68.

MacDonald, B. J. (1998). Issues in therapy with gay and lesbian couples. *Journal of Sex & Marital Therapy, 24*, 165-190.

Ossana, S.M. (2000). Relationship and couples counseling. In R.M. Perez, K.A. DeBord, & K.J. Bieschke (Eds.), *Handbook of counseling and psychotherapy with lesbian, gay, and bisexual clients* (pp. 275-302). Washington, DC: American Psychological Association.

Pardie, L., & Herb, C. R. (1997). Merger and fusion in lesbian relationships: A problem of diagnosing what's wrong in terms of what's right. *Women & Therapy, 20*(3), 51-61.

Peplau, L.A. (1991). Lesbian and gay relationships. In J. Gonsiorek & J.D. Weinrich (Eds.), *Homosexuality: Research implications for public policy* (pp. 177-196). Newbury Park, CA: Sage.

Peplau, L.A., Cochran, S.D., & Mays, V.M. (1997). A national survey of the intimate relationships of African American lesbians and gay men: A look at commitment, satisfaction, sexual behavior, and HIV disease. In B. Greene (Ed.), *Ethnic and cultural diversity among lesbians and gay men* (pp. 11-38). Thousand Oaks, CA: Sage Publications.

Testa, R.J., Kinder, B.N., & Ironson, G. (1987). Heterosexual bias in the perception of loving relationships of gay males and lesbians. *Journal of Sex Research, 23,* 163-172.

Zacks, E., Green, R., & Marrow, J. (1988). Comparing lesbian and heterosexual couples on the circumplex model: An initial investigation. *Family Process, 27,* 471-484.

Young Sexual Minority Women's Perceptions of Cross-Generational Friendships with Older Lesbians

Jeanne L. Stanley

SUMMARY. Perspectives on cross-generational friendships with older lesbians were explored using informal group interviews with two groups of young sexual minority women (N = 16), ages 15 to 25. A majority of the participants were women of color; all were regular members of weekly discussion groups at two lesbian, gay, bisexual and transgendered centers on the East Coast. About half of the young women were interested in having friendships with older lesbians, citing the importance of such relationships for helping younger women cope with coming out, providing a sense of community, and serving as role models and mentors. Others were less interested in becoming friends with older lesbians, citing the generation gap as being an insurmountable obstacle. The participants also perceived that many older lesbians were not interested in cross-gen-

Jeanne L. Stanley, PhD, is Coordinator of the Master's Program in Psychological Services at the University of Pennsylvania. Her research, clinical, and training interests are in the areas of friendship and social support systems, training services for professionals working with people with disabilities and their care providers, and the provision of psychological services to lesbian, gay, bisexual and transgender individuals.

Address correspondence to: Jeanne Stanley, PhD, Graduate Program in Psychological Services, Graduate School of Education, University of Pennsylvania, Philadelphia, PA 19104-3246 (E-mail: jstanley@gse.upenn.edu).

[Haworth co-indexing entry note]: "Young Sexual Minority Women's Perceptions of Cross-Generational Friendships with Older Lesbians." Stanley, Jeanne L. Co-published simultaneously in *Journal of Lesbian Studies* (Harrington Park Press, an imprint of The Haworth Press, Inc.) Vol. 6, No. 1, 2002, pp. 139-148; and: *Lesbian Love and Relationships* (ed: Suzanna M. Rose) Harrington Park Press, an imprint of The Haworth Press, Inc., 2002, pp. 139-148. Single or multiple copies of this article are available for a fee from The Haworth Document Delivery Service [1-800-HAWORTH, 9:00 a.m. - 5:00 p.m. (EST). E-mail address: getinfo@haworthpressinc.com].

139

erational friendships. Ways to create opportunities for forming cross-generational friendships were identified. *[Article copies available for a fee from The Haworth Document Delivery Service: 1-800-HAWORTH. E-mail address: <getinfo@haworthpressinc.com> Website: <http://www.haworthPress.com> © 2002 by The Haworth Press, Inc. All rights reserved.]*

KEYWORDS. Lesbian, bisexual women, sexual minorities, adolescence, young adulthood, coming out, friendship, cross-generational friendship

On the main stage of the Millennium March on Washington, a lesbian activist in her late sixties spoke of her years of marching for lesbian, gay, bisexual and transgender rights. She then paused and specifically addressed the youth in the sea of people, saying: "I'm tired. Now it's your turn." This poignant moment illustrated the changing of the guard that is occurring in the lesbian and gay civil rights movement as the first wave of activists step aside. What we have little knowledge about, however, is how older lesbians are supporting and connecting with the young women to whom they are passing the torch. In the group discussions described below, young sexual minority women (lesbians, bisexuals, and questioning women) explored their perspectives concerning cross-generational friendships with older lesbians. Three questions that were addressed included: (a) What are the characteristics of the friendship networks of young sexual minority women?; (b) Do young lesbian, bisexual, and questioning women desire friendships with older lesbians? Why or why not?; and (c) How could opportunities for cross-generational friendships be created?

LESBIAN FRIENDSHIPS

In general, cross-generational friendships are not as frequent as friendships between individuals of similar ages, or with other commonalties such as gender, ethnicity, race, educational level, income, and religiosity (Fehr, 2000). Once formed, friendships fulfill certain functions. Friendships between heterosexual women have been credited with offering a range of opportunities including support, attachment, assisting in defining one's identity, empathy, stress reduction and guidance (Fehr, 1996; Goodman, 2000). Regardless of sexual orientation, women may also gain an understanding of their sexual self identity through the formation of their friendships with other women (Palladino & Stephenson, 1990).

Similarly, lesbian friendships may be a source of acknowledgement and affirmation in terms of one's identity, romantic relationships, family system, and community connection in a society that is more likely to denounce than to support these women (Slater & Mencher, 1991). Research on lesbians indicates that support, well-being, self-worth and guidance are important functions of their friendships (Stanley, 1996; Wayment & Peplau, 1995).

Social support systems may also act as a buffer against the lack of acceptance, homophobia, and prejudice from the mainstream culture. For sexual minority youth who are already marginalized, community contact and accessibility of resources is imperative (Nesmith, Burton, & Cosgrove, 1999). Such support decreases the isolation some sexual minority women experience due to rejection from their family-of-origin, particularly for lesbians who are just beginning the coming out process. Friendships may also provide basic information about norms that young lesbians and bisexual women do not learn from their parents or heterosexual peers, such as dating, having a relationship with another woman or coming out issues.

The potential for cross-generational friendships among sexual minority women may be greater than ever. Lesbians of all ages are coming out and are therefore more visible, offering more opportunities for connection. Cross-generational friendships constitute a distinct category of friendships that have unique benefits. Older lesbians who themselves have had similar struggles and feelings can offer acceptance and affirmation to young lesbians and bisexual women. Friendships among women of differing ages may also provide a feeling of community as well as an historical perspective on the sexual minority community.

There is, however, little research regarding cross-generational friendships among sexual minority women. One exception is Rose and Roades (1987), who reported that feminists (both lesbian and heterosexual women) were more likely than nonfeminist heterosexual women to have cross-generational friendships with a woman who was not a family member. These findings suggest that involvement in lesbian and feminist communities might provide more opportunities to form friendships across age than are likely to occur among heterosexuals. Weinstock (1998) calls for more research that offers an understanding of the factors, such as age and life course, in order to better understand the role of friendship for sexual minorities.

Limitations associated with friendships in general also occur within cross-generational friendships. Tensions at times are found among friends, leading to various reactions such as anger, disappointment and conflict (Fehr, 2000). Drawbacks may stem from an unequal basis of reciprocity in the friendship or romantic involvement between friends impacting an existing romantic relationship (Shackelford & Buss, 1996; Stanley, 1996). Divisive, clique-like groupings that sometimes occur in the lesbian community may also serve to

limit friendship, as Esterberg (1997) pointed out: "Instead of seeing communities as places in which people really 'are' alike in some fundamental way, we
may be better off acknowledging that lesbian communities are really overlap-
ping friendship networks, and sometimes exclusive ones at that, with multiple
centers and fuzzy boundaries" (p. 175). Age can operate as a factor that promotes exclusivity within the lesbian community. A "twenty-something" lesbian may feel better understood by a gay man her age than by a lesbian in her
fifties and vice versa.

   Given the lack of information about cross-generational lesbian friendships,
the goal of this project was to conduct an informal exploratory investigation of
what two groups of young sexual minority women thought about the idea of
having friendships with older lesbians.

YOUNG LESBIANS DISCUSS
CROSS-GENERATIONAL FRIENDSHIPS

   Two groups of young lesbian, bisexual and questioning women, ages 15 to
25, took part in semi-structured group interviews held at two different lesbian
and gay youth centers on the East Coast. A total of sixteen women participated,
nine in the first group and seven in the second group. The majority of participants (63%, N = 10) were women of color. The first group, labeled the *Urban
Group,* met once a week for two hours at the youth center and was advertised
as being for "anyone who identifies as a woman and who loves women." Eight
members attended on the day of the interview, including six African American
and two White women. A ninth regular group member, a sixteen-year-old African American lesbian, was interviewed later. Two staff members at the center facilitated the Urban Group. One was an African American lesbian (age
24); the other was a White lesbian graduate student (age 30).

   The second group, labeled the *College Group,* was held at the Lesbian, Gay, Bisexual and Transgendered Center on an Ivy League university campus. The group
met weekly for 90 minutes. The facilitator was the assistant director of the center, a
30-year-old White lesbian. On the day of the interview, seven women were present
ranging in age from 18 to 25. Six were enrolled in academic programs and one
worked at the university. Two women were African American, two White, one
Asian American, one African and one from Eastern Europe. For both groups, the
women's sexual identity ranged from lesbian to bisexual to questioning.

   The facilitator(s) of each group asked if members were willing to participate in a group interview on cross-generational friendships led by the author, a
35-year-old, White lesbian psychologist. All participants agreed. Due to the

confidential nature of the group, the discussion was not tape recorded; instead, handwritten notes were taken.

Friendship Networks

Participants in both groups stated that they had between eight and ten close friends, on average. This network size was comparable to that found in previous research on lesbians' friendships. Lesbians in Nardi and Sherrod's (1994) survey reported having about 7.5 close friends; similarly, D'Augelli (1989) found that rural lesbians had about 8.5 close friends. Thus, the young sexual minority women studied here had fairly strong friendship networks that possibly were facilitated by involvement in center activities.

Four types of friendships were distinguished based on their degree of closeness. The order was described as "[Big F] Friends, [little f] friends, buddies and then associates. For instance, as one woman was describing her friendship network, three other women chimed in at the same time, asking "is that [friendship] with a small 'f' or a big 'F'?" Others nodded in agreement at the distinction: Big F friends were the ones who "are there for you and you take care of each other no matter what." Friends with a small "f" were those you connected with once or twice a week. Buddies were occasional contacts; associates were those you connected with only at certain times of the year.

Same-sex friendships tended to be the norm, but a few women indicated having a gay or heterosexual man as a close friend. All but one woman had both lesbian and bisexual women friends in their network. Participants described feeling disconnected from formerly close heterosexual friends who did not know that they were lesbian, bisexual, or questioning their sexual orientation. As they became more open about their sexual orientation, the young women indicated being more likely to seek out other sexual minority women as friends. Sexual minority friends were cited as being more helpful and open than heterosexual friends to issues regarding sexual identity. Women in both groups described having friends of different races, but several of the African American women mentioned the importance of having same-race friendships in order to be able to discuss issues unique to women of color.

Interest in Cross-Generational Friendships

Merriam-Webster's dictionary (1993) defines generational as "the average span of time between the birth of parents and that of their offspring." A minimum age difference of 15 years would be necessary for a friendship to be considered cross-generational. Most participants indicated endorsing this definition. One young woman expanded the definition to include the importance of experiencing different historical and social contexts. She stated: "There is a difference in the social appeal of homosexuality for someone who is 16 and out now, compared to someone who is 46 and out years ago . . . there are obvious changes in society's structure and how people's lives are laid out, but also there are some similar experiences." She continued: "There are obvious differences [between younger and older lesbians]–economically, socially. Like, we can use a computer to get to gay resources anytime or we can think about how gender changes." However, for other participants a five year age difference warranted the cross-generational label. One woman described a friend who was four years older as being "much older," because the friend had graduated college and now had a full-time job.

About half of all participants expressed an interest in having friendships with older lesbians, including six members of the Urban Group and two members of the College Group. These women believed that cross-generational friendships could provide a sense of connection. The other eight participants expressed ambivalence about having friendships with older lesbians. Although they wanted more adult lesbian mentors and role models, particularly in terms of "out" lesbian and bisexual female faculty, they did not see this type of relationship as needing to translate into a friendship.

The participants identified five potential benefits linked to cross-generational friendships with older lesbians. First, older lesbians would be able to provide support and advice related to issues unique to being a sexual minority such as coming out issues and dating someone of the same sex. Most of the participants mentioned that they could not ask their parents or their heterosexual peers about areas related to their sexual identity. Acceptance was a second perceived benefit. Some participants believed that cross-generational friends would be more likely to encourage you to "be who you are," whereas same-age friends more often wanted to dictate specifically how a peer should act and respond.

A third benefit that might be provided by friendships with older lesbians was a sense of community and shared history. As a seventeen-year-old African American youth stated: "Whatever they [older lesbians] felt back then, I feel now. I have more resources than they did, but in common we have self-esteem issues, coming out issues, homophobia to deal with because of our gayness." This supports Nesmith, Burton, and Cosgrove's (1999) findings that sexual minority youth benefit from reciprocal social support systems with other sexual minorities in the community.

Fourth, having older role models was viewed as an asset. One example given was that of Ruth Ellis, an African American lesbian from Detroit who lived to be more than 100. Many participants had been inspired by the documentary of her life entitled: *Living with Pride: Ruth C. Ellis at 100* by Yvonne

Welbon (1999). Fifth, participants also believed that cross-generational friendships would benefit older lesbians. One young woman stated: "An older person might think 'I never had this when I was younger.' I want to give back so they don't feel stranded and alone."

Other young sexual minority women were indifferent to the idea of cross-generational friendships. In both groups, some participants responded with shrugs regarding their interest in friendships with older lesbians. In general, these women thought cross-generational friendships were useless because of the "generation gap." One nineteen-year-old African American youth said, and others agreed: "We already got a mother, we don't need another." They said they did not want another adult commenting on their choices and decisions. Others believed their day-to-day experiences were so different from those of older lesbians that they would have little in common. Participants discussed how difficult it was to see older lesbians as friends rather than mentors. Mentoring was described as more hierarchical and one-sided.

Most participants perceived that older lesbians had little interest in forming friendships with younger women. A woman from the Urban Group commented that older lesbians think, "They have nothing in common with us," or "I don't see how I fit in with you, I don't know what to do, I have nothing to offer you." Others believed older lesbians were not interested in "keeping up with the changes" or were intimidated about the issues young sexual minority women face. One seventeen-year-old African American woman commented: "They get scared if they hear about drug issues, sex workers, abuse or domestic violence that the youth are experiencing and they get flipped out about what's going on. They get jaded. We have real problems and real issues because we are real people. We are dealing with other things than just being gay and we need help with more than just schoolwork." Some suggested that older lesbians who are closeted about their sexual orientation avoid gay youth "because we amplify their gayness."

In addition, older lesbians were seen as avoiding young women because they do not want to be in the role of an authority figure for the youth. As one young woman indicated: "When adults mirror back what they did in their lives, they then have fears about what we are doing. They then want to tell us what to do with our lives. But then they pull away because they don't want to be a cop. They don't want to cross that line. They didn't like being told [what to do], so they don't like telling us what to do. They feel like it's not their place." Last, participants hypothesized that older lesbians avoided connecting with younger women because of what they called "the chicken hawk thing," referring to the stereotype that adult lesbians are out to seduce and take advantage of youth.

Creating Opportunities for Cross-Generational Friendship

Several participants were eager to create opportunities for cross-generational friendships and some had been involved in projects at their respective centers to facilitate those relationships. One young woman described her ideas for building bridges across the generations, saying that it was important "to build on our similar experiences and feelings" by creating opportunities that were not awkward or intimidating to either the youth or the adults. To support her recommendation, she described a new program at the Urban Center aimed at getting adult volunteers to feel comfortable volunteering at the center. The program was called the "Volunteer Posse." First, as with all volunteers, the youth leadership group interviewed potential volunteers. They were looking for volunteers who were interested in being involved with young people and who would be respectful toward them. Volunteers who were selected were then paired with a younger "buddy" for a three-week period. After three weeks, a new buddy was assigned to the volunteer. This procedure was aimed at helping adult volunteers feel more comfortable working with different youth. Before the Volunteer Posse was established, potential volunteers would come in and "feel like they are going into someone's bedroom when they shouldn't. Adult volunteers feel threatened because it is threatening to come into the center because they do not know their role. They want to make a difference but they don't know how. They aren't as comfortable as they thought they were." The Posse was working well in assisting older volunteers to feel more at ease.

Women at the College Center described another program aimed at linking younger and older women. The program, which had been in operation for the past two years, linked "mentors" (predominantly lesbians who were seniors and graduate students) with undergraduate sexual minority women. Eight lesbian and bisexual women undergraduates were paired with mentors in the first year and twelve in the second year. Participants rated the program as being highly successful at providing social support.

Other young women suggested that older lesbians could connect by listening to them and finding out what issues affected them, such as current political and educational issues, instead of assuming they already know all the issues. Older lesbians also were advised to take the time necessary to connect with younger lesbians rather than "force your way" into conversations and events. Finally, educating both young and older women about what they have to offer each other was seen as a way to create opportunities for friendship.

CONCLUSION

Audre Lorde (1984) wrote: "The question of lesbian friendship is central to the building of lesbian community and realizing a lesbian vision." Cross-generational friendships and connections are an integral part of this vision. This study indicated that sexual minority youth have different perceptions of what signifies cross-generational friendships, ranging from a period of a few years, to a few decades. The study also found that half the sexual minority female youths were interested in having friendships with older lesbians, particularly because of the benefits related to support, acceptance, advice, community building, and role models. The other half was ambivalent or not interested in crossing what they perceived as an insurmountable generation gap. Disinterest may be related to the developmental processes of adolescence and young adulthood where emphasis is placed on understanding one's own self through socialization and intimacy through one's peer group. Successful examples of cross-generational friendships in the centers that participated in the study offered positive models for how other school/university programming, youth groups, and sexual minority community centers can foster opportunities for connection across the age span for sexual minority women. Audre Lorde's call for realizing a lesbian vision cannot belong to one age group; rather, women of all ages must be included.

REFERENCES

D'Augelli, A. R. (1989). Lesbian women in rural helping networks: Exploring informal helping resources. *Women & Therapy, 8*, 119-130.

Esterberg, K. G. (1997). *Lesbian and bisexual identities: Constructing communities, constructing selves.* Philadelphia: Temple University Press.

Fehr, B. A. (1996). *Friendship processes.* Thousand Oaks, CA: Sage Publications.

Fehr, B. A. (2000). The lifecycle of friendship. In C. Hendrick & S. S. Hendrick (Eds.), *Close relationships: A sourcebook* (pp. 71-82). Thousand Oaks, CA: Sage Publications.

Goodman, E. (2000). *I know just what you mean: The power of friendship in women's lives.* New York: Simon & Schuster.

Lorde, A. (1984). *Sister outsider: Essays and speeches.* Freedom, CA: Crossing Press.

Merriam-Webster's collegiate dictionary (1993). Springfield, MA: Merriam-Webster.

Nardi, P.M., & Sherrod, D. (1994). Friendships in the lives of gay men and lesbians. *Journal of Social and Personal Relationships, 11*, 185-199.

Nesmith, A. A., Burton, D. L. & Cosgrove, T. J. (1999). Gay, lesbian, and bisexual youth and young adults: Social support in their own words. *Journal of Homosexuality, 37* (1), 95-108.

Palladino, D., & Stephenson, Y. (1990). Perceptions of the sexual self: Their impact on relationships between lesbian and heterosexual women. *Women & Therapy, 9* (3), 231-253.

Rose, S., & Roades, L. (1987). Feminism and women's friendships. *Psychology of Women Quarterly, 11*, 243-254.

Shackelford, T. K., & Buss, D. M. (1996). Betrayal in mateships, friendships, and coalitions. *Personality and Social Psychology Bulletin, 22*, 1151-1164.

Slater, S., & Mencher, J. (1991). The lesbian family life cycle: A contextual approach. *American Journal of Orthopsychiatry, 61*, 372-382.

Stanley, J. L. (1996). The lesbian's experience of friendship. In J. S. Weinstock & E. D. Rothblum (Eds.), *Lesbian friendships: For ourselves and each other* (pp. 39-59). New York: New York University Press.

Wayment, H. A., & Peplau, L. A. (1995). Social support and well-being among lesbian and heterosexual women: A structural modeling approach. *Personality & Social Psychology Bulletin, 21*(11), 1189-1199.

Weinstock, J. S. (1998). Lesbian, gay, and bisexual adolescents. In A. R. D'Augelli & C. J. Patterson (Eds.), *Lesbian, gay, and bisexual identities in families: Psychological Perspectives* (pp. 122-153). New York: Oxford University Press.

Welbon, Y. (Producer and Director). (1999). *Living with pride: Ruth C. Ellis @ 100* [videotape]. (Available from Our Film Works Inc., P.O. Box 267848, Chicago, IL 60626)

Building Bridges:
Examining Lesbians'
and Heterosexual Women's
Close Friendships with Each Other

Jacqueline S. Weinstock
Lynne A. Bond

Jacqueline S. Weinstock (PhD, 1993, University of Vermont) is Assistant Professor of Integrated Professional Studies at the University of Vermont where she teaches in the Human Development and Family Systems Studies Program. Her research explores lesbian, gay, bisexual, and transgender (LGBT) developmental and relationship issues, including friendship, and the impact of oppression on development. Among her recent publications is a forthcoming chapter in the 3rd edition of *Teaching a Psychology of People* that offers suggestions for psychologists concerning how to integrate LGBT issues into psychology curricula. Professor Weinstock received the "Award for Public Service" (2000) from the American College Personnel Association's Standing Committee for Lesbian, Gay, Bisexual, and Transgendered Awareness, and was given the "Outstanding LGBT Faculty Member Award" by her university's LGBT community.

Lynne A. Bond, PhD, is Professor of Psychology at the University of Vermont, where she has been on the faculty since 1976 and served as Dean of the Graduate College from 1986-1995. Professor Bond earned her PhD in psychology from Tufts University. Her work promotes individual, family, and community development and emphasizes the social, cognitive, and gender development of women and children. Dr. Bond also is President of the Vermont Conferences on the Primary Prevention of Psychopathology, Inc., and has edited seven volumes in its publication series. She is a Fellow of the Community Psychology Division and a member of the Developmental Psychology Division and the Society for the Psychology of Women of the American Psychological Association.

Address correspondence to the authors at the University of Vermont, C-150 Living & Learning Center, Burlington, VT 05405 (E-mail: jsweinst@zoo.uvm.edu or lbond@zoo.uvm.edu).

[Haworth co-indexing entry note]: "Building Bridges: Examining Lesbians' and Heterosexual Women's Close Friendships with Each Other." Weinstock, Jacqueline S., and Lynne A. Bond. Co-published simultaneously in *Journal of Lesbian Studies* (Harrington Park Press, an imprint of The Haworth Press, Inc.) Vol. 6, No. 1, 2002, pp. 149-161; and: *Lesbian Love and Relationships* (ed: Suzanna M. Rose) Harrington Park Press, an imprint of The Haworth Press, Inc., 2002, pp. 149-161. Single or multiple copies of this article are available for a fee from The Haworth Document Delivery Service [1-800-HAWORTH, 9:00 a.m. - 5:00 p.m. (EST). E-mail address: getinfo@haworthpressinc.com].

149

SUMMARY. Friendships between lesbians and heterosexual women were explored using a sample of 47 mostly White women (23 lesbians and 24 heterosexual women), ages 18 to 25, that reported at least one close lesbian-heterosexual woman friendship. A majority of participants indicated that friendships between lesbians and heterosexual women had both uniquely positive and negative aspects that could be attributed to the difference in sexual identity. Positive aspects included socio-emotional benefits, opportunities for learning, and societal benefits. Negative aspects included anxiety about sexuality, doubts regarding mutual understanding, clashes of perspectives and experience, and societal stressors. Implications of the findings for challenging current social inequities associated with sexual identities were explored. *[Article copies available for a fee from The Haworth Document Delivery Service: 1-800-HAWORTH. E-mail address: <getinfo@haworthpressinc.com> Website: <http://www.HaworthPress.com> © 2002 by The Haworth Press, Inc. All rights reserved.]*

KEYWORDS. Lesbian, friendship, same-sex friendship, women's friendships, young adults, heterosexual women, sexual orientation, sexual identity

Who are your closest friends? Most friends are quite similar on a variety of identity dimensions including biological sex, race, class, and age. Still, some friendships cross identity lines. In this research, we focused on exploring the experiences of friendship between young lesbians and heterosexual women. We examined the positive and negative aspects described as being unique to these friendships, including their perceived benefits and challenges, factors that appeared to facilitate or hinder their development and maintenance, and the potential these relationships held for redressing current social inequities associated with sexual identities.

RESEARCH ON FRIENDSHIP

Lesbian and heterosexual adult women typically value friendships and experience them as important contributors to their health and development. They also tend to form and sustain friendships with others who are similar along a variety of dimensions, including socioeconomic class, race, ethnicity, age, biological sex, gender, and life cycle phase (see, e.g., Blieszner & Adams, 1992;

Fehr, 1996; O'Connor, 1992). This pattern suggests that adults also may be drawn to particular friendships because of similar sexual identities, but this issue rarely has been considered in research on heterosexual friendship (Weinstock, 1998; Werking, 1997). In contrast, sexual identity has been a focus of investigations of lesbians' and gay men's friendships almost to the exclusion of other identity dimensions. Lesbians and gay men overwhelmingly report more same-sexuality friends in general and more such close friends than any other type of friend (Nardi, 1999; Weinstock, 1998).

Similar identity friendships may form, in part, as a consequence of the tendency for adults to live and work in segregated settings and/or to engage in activities that tend to bring homogeneous groups of people together (Blieszner & Adams, 1992). Identities and experiences that reflect similarities in terms of access to power also provide a basis for friendships to develop. For instance, sexual minority group members may seek out others like themselves because those friendships help relieve the stress associated with living in a heterosexist society. Interestingly, people who are members of oppressed groups are more likely than those in privileged groups to have heterogeneous friendship networks (Blieszner & Adams, 1992). People in the majority group have higher status in most societies and they are less likely to choose someone with a lesser status as a friend. In addition, oppressed group members are more likely to be both in contact and familiar with the majority culture (out of necessity if not choice) than the reverse, providing more opportunities for forming such friendships.

Friendships across lesbian-heterosexual sexual identities have been of interest to lesbian and women's studies scholars and activists, who have looked to the potential of women's friendships for furthering women's individual and community development, as well as the aims of feminism (e.g., Hall & Rose, 1996; O'Connor, 1992; Raymond, 1986). Although not the dominant pattern, friendships across sexual identities do exist, as reflected in both research reports and personal stories (e.g., Daly, 1996; O'Boyle & Thomas, 1996; Price, 1999; Weinstock & Rothblum, 1996). The limited research available suggests that lesbians and heterosexual women face special issues in their friendships with each other. For example, Palladino and Stephenson (1990) argued that it is likely that erotic feelings will occur in friendships between lesbians and heterosexual women, given the connectedness of many female-female relationships. They conclude that lesbians and heterosexual women need to define and accept their own sexual selves if they are to become friends. Kolodner (1992) found that heterosexual women reported different experiences in their friendships with other heterosexual women than with lesbians, with more romantic love, total intimacy, support and acceptance in their same-sexuality friendships than in their other-sexuality friendships.

O'Boyle and Thomas (1996) identified barriers to close friendships between lesbians and heterosexual women based on separate focus group interviews. One barrier was the concern by the lesbians that heterosexual women might be wary of any physical intimacy lesbians express or of conversations about their sexual relationships. The lesbians noted their tendency to restrict such behaviors in their friendships with heterosexual women, and heterosexual women reported less personal disclosure and discussion of their sexual relationships with their lesbian than their heterosexual women friends. But the most significant barrier identified by O'Boyle and Thomas (1996) was lesbians' oppression, which inhibited discussions between lesbians and heterosexual women and, therefore, allowed negative stereotypes to persist. O'Boyle and Thomas (1996) argued that both lesbians and heterosexual women have to overcome a profound sense of difference. To do so, heterosexual women must confront their own heterosexism, whereas lesbians have to focus on aspects of their heterosexual friends' identities and interests that are shared.

There are both potential benefits and challenges to forming friendships across sexual identities. Such friendships may provide mutual affirmation and support. Alternatively, they also may reflect and replicate existing social inequities and stereotypes regarding women's sexual identities. In the present study, lesbians' and heterosexual women's reports of their experiences in lesbian-heterosexual friendships were explored with the aim of furthering our understanding of and ability to support women's friendships across diverse sexual identities.

METHOD

Participants

In the context of a larger survey, 109 women provided their perceptions of friendships across sexual identities. Almost 90% of the respondents were Caucasian undergraduate students attending a small, New England university. Fifty of the 109 women identified as heterosexual but did not have a close cross-sexuality friendship and twelve women indicated having a close bisexual friend, but no close lesbian friend. These respondents were excluded from the current analysis. The results reported here were derived from the remaining 47 female respondents, aged 18-25 years, including: (a) 23 self-identified lesbians who had at least one close heterosexual woman friend; and (b) 24 self-identified heterosexual women who had at least one close lesbian friend.

Measures

The survey, constructed by the authors, asked participants to provide basic demographic information, including sexual identity, as well as to indicate how many close female friends they currently had who were lesbian, bisexual, or heterosexual. They were then asked to describe, in writing, "exciting, productive, or particularly joyful aspects" and, subsequently, "stressful, draining, or uncomfortable aspects" of having a friend with a different (specified) sexual identity.

Procedure

Over a two-year period, surveys were distributed to several introductory psychology and human development courses as well as upper level, small seminar classes at a New England university. Completion of the surveys was voluntary and anonymous; in some courses, class time was made available for survey completion. In addition, surveys were distributed directly to several lesbian, gay, bisexual, and transgender-related organizations. Surveys also were collected at one annual Pride Event in the New England area.

Data Analyses

Qualitative data analyses followed Tesch's (1990) model of the "discovery of regularities." Two coders (the authors) independently examined the responses to each survey question separately within each sexual identity to identify principal themes; attempts were made to note as many distinct themes as possible. There was strong consensus between the coders in terms of existing themes. There was also considerable commonality in the overarching themes used by women with different sexual identities. Thus, one common set of 36 themes was used to code all responses, including 21 positive themes and 15 negative themes (see Tables 1 and 2, respectively). Subsequently, we coded each survey in terms of whether or not the respondent referred to each of the 36 themes. Overall inter-rater agreement (Kappa) was 85% (calculated on 15% of the data). The themes were later grouped into four major positive and five major negative categories.

RESULTS AND DISCUSSION

As expected, the majority of participants indicated that friendships between lesbians and heterosexual women had both uniquely positive and negative aspects that were attributable to the difference in sexual identity.

TABLE 1. Percentage of Participants Identifying Uniquely Positive Themes of Friendships Between Lesbians and Heterosexual Women by Sexual Orientation[1]

Positive Themes	Sexual Orientation		
	Lesbians (n = 23)	Heterosexual Women (n = 24)	Total (N = 47)
A. Socio-Emotional Benefits	**78%**	**54%**	**66%**
1. Appreciation for friend	61	17	38
2. Interesting interactions	17	25	21
3. Honest communication	9	33	21
4. No sexual tension/complications	17	0	9
5. Understanding/open-mindedness	4	17	11
6. Physical/erotic intimacy	9	8	9
7. Boost status/trendy	4	0	2
8. Less competition	0	4	2
9. Challenges of differing identities	0	4	2
B. Learning Opportunities	**61**	**58**	**60**
1. Education (general)	35	33	34
2. Gain perspectives on lifestyle	22	33	28
3. Break down stereotypes	17	17	17
4. New perspectives on love	9	17	13
5. Develop more understanding of women	4	8	6
6. Examine own sexuality	0	8	4
7. Be exposed to new people	0	8	4
8. Learn about heterosexism	0	4	2
9. Become more open-minded	0	4	2
C. Societal Benefits	**13**	**0**	**6**
1. Break down barriers	9	0	4
2. Build community/allies	9	0	4
D. None	**22**	**25**	**23**

[1] Columns do not add to 100% due to multiple responses.

Positive Themes of Friendships

As shown in Table 1, most participants (77%) responded positively when asked to identify the "exciting, productive, or particularly joyful aspects" of having a friendship between a lesbian and a heterosexual woman. Twenty-one positive themes were identified and coded. The themes then were grouped into four major categories, including: (a) socio-emotional benefits of these relationships and friends, (b) opportunities for learning about oneself, others, and the world, (c) constructive benefits to society (lesbian respondents only), and (d) no uniquely positive aspects.

Socio-emotional benefits. Overall, a majority of participants (66%) indicated there were clear socio-emotional benefits associated with the friendships being studied. A foremost benefit according to more lesbians (61%) than heterosexual women (17%) was that friendships across sexual identities provided an *appreciation for who each friend is* (e.g., "being able to love each other for who we are"). This appreciation appeared to offer lesbians support during the coming out process and helped the development of a positive lesbian identity more generally. For example, one lesbian reported, "My friends give me the courage to come out and be who I am," while another noted that her friends "have been supportive and absolutely accepting" and that this was "wonderful for my coming out experience."

A second frequently cited socio-emotional benefit was *interesting interactions.* About 21% of participants reported that these friendships were particularly stimulating due to the friend's different perspective. *Honest communication* was a third benefit identified by heterosexual women (33%), but less often by lesbians (9%). In general, the heterosexual women appreciated having the lesbian friend's trust and openness. A fourth benefit, according to 17% of lesbians but none of the heterosexual women, was the *absence of sexual tension* in the friendship.

Five other socio-emotional benefits mentioned less frequently included the following: the unusual *understanding or open-mindedness* the friend provided; *physical or erotic intimacy* in the friendship; the *boost in status* provided by having a trendy cross-sexuality friendship (lesbians only); *less competition* for dates and relationships (heterosexual women only); and the opportunity to work through *the challenges of differing identities* (heterosexual women only) (11, 9, 2, 2, and 2 percent of respondents, respectively).

Opportunities to learn. A majority of respondents (60%) identified at least one of the nine sub-themes comprising the opportunities to learn category as being a positive aspect of their cross-sexuality friendships. According to both groups, the dominant direction of learning was for heterosexual women to gain knowledge from their lesbian friends. The two most frequently cited themes were the benefits of *education* (in general; 34%) and *learning about another lifestyle* (28%). Typical of the heterosexual women were comments such as: "You see a different culture," "You get a different perspective on things," and "I seemed to get a better view and understanding of being gay." Similarly, lesbians also noted how these friends "share different viewpoints" and "get a different perspective on life."

The three next most often mentioned learning opportunities pertained to *breaking down stereotypes and prejudices* (17%), *gaining new perspectives on love* (13%), and *developing more understanding of women* (6%). Breaking down stereotypes related specifically to images of romantic and sexual relations. One lesbian noted learning from her heterosexual friend "how our lives are more similar and different than we sometimes think," whereas a heterosexual woman reported: "being a close friend of a lesbian I was not as fearful of what 'they' were like. I found that lesbians have similar thoughts or questions/concerns about what to do in a relationship (similar to heterosexual couples)." In terms of gaining new perspectives on love, one heterosexual woman reported that her friend "taught me a lot about the love that grows between people [independent] of their sex and sexual preference." Similarly, one lesbian noted that "it's always interesting to see how much our relationships with our respective partners are so different yet similar." A small proportion of respondents felt that the friendships expanded their understanding and appreciation of women, including themselves (i.e., the theme: more understanding of women).

Four less often mentioned themes of learning opportunities were cited only by heterosexual women. These included: the chance *to examine their own sexuality, be exposed to new people, learn more about heterosexism,* and *become more open-minded* (4, 4, 2, and 2 percent respectively). These findings imply that the friendships provide a constellation of opportunities for personal growth for some heterosexual women.

Societal benefits. A third category of benefits, noted only among lesbian respondents (13%), focused on the ways friendships across sexual identity have constructive effects on society itself, specifically by *breaking down barriers* (social and personal) that typically keep people with different sexual identities apart, and *building community/allies* (9% of lesbians supported each).

None. About 23 percent of survey respondents either did not identify any particular benefit of friendships between lesbians and heterosexual women or they noted that the benefits were not related to the friends' sexual identities.

In sum, three major benefits were associated with friendships between lesbians and heterosexual women among a sample of women who successfully had established such relationships, including socio-emotional benefits, learning opportunities, and positive societal effects. The benefits, however, also reflected conditions that serve to facilitate or inhibit the development of such friendships (see also O'Boyle & Thomas, 1996). If heterosexual women do not develop an understanding of what it is like to be a lesbian in a heterosexist society, they may be less able to break through stereotypes to form a friendship across sexuality or to reach a deep appreciation for who the lesbian friend is as an individual. Conversely, if lesbians do not feel appreciated for who they are, they may be less likely to engage in friendships that require them to educate the friend (e.g., Stanley, 1996). The reported emphasis on the heterosexual friend's learning described here may not only limit the development of closeness in these friendships but may also reflect the impact of heterosexism on both the individual and the friendship.

Negative Themes of Friendships

As shown in Table 2, participants described fifteen negative themes when asked to describe "stressful, draining, or uncomfortable aspects" of having a

TABLE 2. Percentage of Participants Identifying Uniquely Negative Themes of Friendships Between Lesbians and Heterosexual Women by Sexual Orientation[1]

Negative Themes	Sexual Orientation		
	Lesbians (n = 23)	Heterosexual Women (n = 24)	Total (N = 47)
A. Anxiety About Sexuality	**43%**	**46%**	**45%**
1. Concern about sexual attraction	17	29	23
2. Discomfort with sexuality/relationship expression	17	8	13
3. Feeling devalued due to sexual identity	13	0	6
4. Fear of misinterpretation of intentions	8	0	4
5. Discomfort with physical affection	4	4	4
6. General discomfort regarding sexuality	0	8	4
B. Limitations of Understanding	**65**	**8**	**36**
1. Inability to understand	43	4	23
2. Lack of appreciation	22	0	11
3. Inability to communicate	9	4	6
C. Clash of Perspectives	**43**	**13**	**28**
1. Heterosexual privilege	22	8	15
2. Burden of educating friend	17	0	9
3. Political differences	13	0	6
D. Societal Level Stressors	**22**	**17**	**19**
1. Negative responses of network	22	13	17
2. Mislabeling by others	4	8	6
E. None	**9**	**46**	**26**

[1] Columns do not add to 100% due to multiple responses.

friendship between a lesbian and a heterosexual woman. Themes were grouped into five categories, including: (a) *anxiety about sexuality,* (b) *limitations of understanding,* (c) *clash of perspectives,* (d) *societal level stressors* resulting from others' reactions to the friendship, and (e) *none* (i.e., no uniquely negative aspects).

Anxiety about sexuality was the category of negative themes that was most frequently cited by both groups of women (45%). Of the six themes in this category, *concern about a possible or actual sexual attraction* between friends was mentioned most frequently (23%), with heterosexual women reporting this more frequently (29%) than lesbians (17%). Next was *discomfort with sexuality or relationship expression,* with 17% of lesbians indicating some discomfort when expressing their sexuality around their heterosexual women friends and 8% of heterosexual women reporting discomfort with the friend's sexuality. That is, for both lesbians and heterosexual women reporting this theme, the concern was with the lesbian's expression of her sexuality and/or relationship. Two additional themes emerged from the lesbian respondents only, *feeling devalued due to sexual identity* (13%) and *fear of misinterpretation of intentions* (8%). The two least frequently cited themes were *discomfort with physical affection* (4% of both groups), and *general discomfort regarding sexuality* (8% heterosexual women only). Taken together, these findings indicate that sexuality related issues might be major barriers to a close lesbian-heterosexual woman friendship. Indeed, both women may be "on guard" or refrain from being "too friendly" in an effort to avoid the development of attraction or any miscommunication or misinterpretation in this regard.

Limitations of understanding. This category was cited by a majority of lesbians (65%) but only a few heterosexual women (8%). Within this category, the most frequently cited theme was perceived or actual *inability to understand* each other across sexual orientation. About 43% of lesbians expressed this concern, compared to 4% of heterosexual women. Lesbians specifically mentioned the differences in daily experiences both within and beyond romantic and sexual relationships they and their friend experienced, as well as the heterosexual woman's limited understanding of their experience of oppression as lesbians. As one lesbian respondent reported, "It's very hard for me to discuss extremely personal feelings about gender identity and sexual orientation with straight friends. I never feel that I will be met with acceptance or understanding." The second most often mentioned limitation of understanding pertained to *lack of appreciation.* Nearly 22% of lesbians indicated feeling unappreciated in their friendships with heterosexual women, but none of the heterosexual women endorsed this theme. Last, *inability to communicate* was mentioned by a small percentage of participants (6%) as being difficult in cross-sexuality friendships. Overall, the limitations of understanding in these friendships constrained women's willingness to open up with one another about their feelings, opinions, and behaviors and limited opportunities to develop an open and supportive relationship.

Clash of perspectives. Another negative category endorsed by 28% of participants pertained to the clash of perspectives that such friendships might engender due to the discordant social/political perspectives and experiences of the two groups. Lesbians more often than heterosexual women mentioned this category (43% vs. 13%, respectively). Three specific clashes were identified. Most often mentioned was the challenge of dealing with *heterosexual privilege* (22% of lesbians and 8% of heterosexual women), with lesbians reporting difficulty in dealing with the friend's heterosexist attitudes or behaviors and the sense of otherness that this caused. Two other types of strains (cited by lesbians only) included the *burden of educating the friend* about issues that concerned them as lesbians (17%) and *political differences* in commitment to and style of politics (including anti-heterosexism politics, gender role expression, feminism, and other values) (13%). One lesbian suggested, "Sometimes heterosexual friends just *don't* get the political implications of the isolation and non-identity a lesbian can feel in the midst of a very heterosexual world." Another explained, "I hate feeling like an educator to my heterosexual woman friends; I often need to help them confront their heterosexism."

Societal level stressors. Stress was cited by 19% of respondents as another negative aspect of cross-sexuality friendships. The most often cited theme within this category was *negative responses of network* (17%). Participants worried about the friend or themselves feeling ostracized or devalued by the other's larger friendship or family community. Stress associated with integrating the friendship into one or the other's social network was mentioned specifically: "[it's a strain] not being able to attend functions together because I may not be accepted there," and "having my friend be uncomfortable around my other gay friends [is difficult]." A second infrequently mentioned theme was *mislabeling by others,* with some (6%) fearing that others would mistakenly label their own sexual identity as identical to their friend's.

None. About 26% of participants indicated there were no uniquely negative aspects to their friendships. Many fewer lesbians (9%) than heterosexual women (45%) indicated no negatives.

In sum, participants described several uniquely negative aspects of friendships between lesbians and heterosexual women. The findings indicate the complexities of women's friendship due to the differing histories and perspectives of the friends. Two negative categories, anxiety about sexual attraction and social stressors, reflected the larger context of heterosexism as well as the heterosexual romance paradigm (O'Boyle & Thomas, 1996; Rose, 1996; Werking, 1997). Heterosexual women sometimes erroneously presumed that lesbians would be attracted to a same-sex friend. In response, some lesbians felt discomfort displaying or sharing their own romantic feelings and relationships. If both lesbians and heterosexual women collude in removing the lesbian's sexuality from the friendship—for example, by refraining from talking about same-sex attractions or romantic relationships, or touching a same-sex partner in the presence of a friend—both are acting out of and reinforcing heterosexism. Our data suggest that heterosexism complicates the development of a trusting, open, or guilt-free relationship. As heterosexual women develop greater understanding of heterosexism, however, they are likely to become stronger and better friends to lesbians.

CONCLUSION

Our findings indicate that for young White college women, friendships across sexual identities offer valued socio-emotional and learning opportunities as well as societal benefits. In addition, the responses of lesbians and heterosexual women with cross-sexuality friendships indicated considerable overlap in experiences and perspectives. Yet there are challenges that also stand in the way of such friendships. Friendships across such boundaries are rarely simple or easy. The friendships may both reflect and reinforce existing social realities and structures (O'Connor, 1992). Indeed, the challenges identified by both groups of women are similar to those reported by women who work across other socially constructed boundaries of power (see, e.g., Hall & Rose, 1996; O'Connor, 1992; Wilson & Russell, 1996). At the same time, friendships across these boundaries offer a potential site for struggling against such constraints to reach an appreciation for the deep and diverse value of these friendships. For lesbians and heterosexual women alike, the work required seems well worth the effort.

ACKNOWLEDGMENTS

The authors would like to thank the survey participants for sharing their thoughts and experiences; Suzanna Rose, editor of this publication, for her specific suggestions and general support for their work; and their friends, colleagues, and students who have shared in many wide-ranging and thought-provoking conversations about friendships across sexual identities.

REFERENCES

Blieszner, R., & Adams, R. G. (1992). *Adult friendship*. Newbury Park, CA: Sage.

Daly, M. (1996) (Ed.). *Surface tension: Love, sex, and politics between lesbians and straight women*. New York: Simon & Schuster.

Fehr, B. (1996). *Friendship processes*. Thousand Oaks, CA: Sage.

Hall, R., & Rose, S. (1996). Friendships between African-American and White lesbians. In J. S. Weinstock & E. D. Rothblum (Eds.), *Lesbians and friendship: For ourselves and each other* (pp. 165-191). New York: New York University Press.

Kolodner, E. M. (1992). *Sexual orientation as a factor in women's friendships: An empirical exploration of intimacy*. Unpublished paper, Yale University, New Haven, CT.

Nardi, P. M. (1999). *Gay men's friendships: Invincible communities*. Chicago: The University of Chicago Press.

Nardi, P. M., & Sherrod, D. (1994). Friendships in the lives of gay men and lesbians. *Journal of Social and Personal Relationships, 11*, 185-199.

O'Boyle, C. G., & Thomas, M. D. (1996). Friendships between lesbian and heterosexual women. In J. S. Weinstock & E. D. Rothblum (Eds.), *Lesbian friendships: For ourselves and each other* (pp. 240-248). New York: New York University Press.

O'Connor, P. (1992). *Friendships between women: A critical review*. New York: The Guilford Press.

Palladino, D., & Stephenson, Y. (1990). Perceptions of the sexual self: Their impact on relationships between lesbian and heterosexual women. *Women & Therapy, 9*, 231-253.

Price, J. (1999). *Navigating differences: Friendships between gay and straight men*. New York: Haworth Press.

Raymond, J. G. (1986). *A passion for friends: Towards a philosophy of female affection*. Boston: Beacon Press.

Rose, S. (1996). Lesbian and gay love scripts. In E. D. Rothblum & L. A. Bond (Eds.), *Preventing heterosexism and homophobia* (pp. 151-173). Thousand Oaks: Sage.

Stanley, J. L. (1996). The lesbian's experience of friendship. In J. S. Weinstock & E. D. Rothblum (Eds.), *Lesbian friendships: For ourselves and each other* (pp. 39-59). New York: New York University Press.

Tesch, R. (1990). *Qualitative research: Analysis types and software tools*. New York: Falmer.

Weinstock, J. S. (1998). Lesbian, gay, bisexual, and transgender friendships in adulthood: Review and analysis. In C. J. Patterson & A. R. D'Augelli (Eds.), *Lesbian, gay, and bisexual identities in families: Psychological perspectives* (pp. 122-153). New York: Oxford University Press.

Weinstock, J. S., & Rothblum, E. D. (Eds.) (1996). *Lesbians and friendship: For ourselves and each other*. New York: New York University Press.

Werking, K. (1997). *We're just good friends: Women and men in nonromantic relationships*. New York: Guilford.

Wilson, M., & Russell, K. (1996). *Divided sisters: Bridging the gap between black women and white women*. New York: Doubleday.

Index

Adolescent friendships, 5-16
  characteristics of sexual-minority
    women's, 7-10
  developmental context of
    passionate, 10-11
  as romantic relationships, 5-6
  sexual identity and, 13-14
  sexual involvements in passionate,
    11-13
  study design, 6-7
Advertisements, personal, 45-51
African American lesbians, social
    class differences and, 65-74
Age
  dating and courtship and, 98,
    104-105
  as factor in friendship formation,
    145. *See also*
    Cross-generational
    friendships
Appearance, physical, group
    membership and, 31-43
Attitudes, changes in, 1-2
Attraction, signs of sexual, 101-102
Autonomy, partner violence and,
    125-126

Battering, partner, 121-127. *See also*
    Partner violence
Body weight issues, 34,35
Butch/femme
  definitions, 46
  descriptions in personal
    advertisements, 45-51
  personal memoir, 75-84
  social history of, 46

(University of) California-Los Angeles,
    53-63
Clinical implications, of dating and
    courtship study, 106-107
College of New Jersey, 65-74
Coming out, physical appearance and,
    31-43
Commitment, 53-63
  factors in, 54-55
  method, 55-57
  results, 57-61
Couples therapy, 129-138
  impact of homophobia, 131-132
  intimacy and merger in lesbian
    relationships, 132-136
Courtship, 85-109. *See also* Dating and
    Courtship
Cross-generational friendships, 139-148
  among lesbians generally, 140-142
  young lesbians' attitudes, 142-146

Dating and courtship, 85-109
  age and, 98, 104-105
  clinical implications of study,
    106-107
  conclusions, 105-107
  developmental issues in, 89-91
  friendship vs. romance in, 100-103
  gender roles and, 88-89,103-104
  method, 92-93
  results and discussion, 93-105
  scripts of, 86-88,93-96
  uniqueness in lesbian, 97-100
Dating experience, 17-29
  characteristics of dating, 22-23
  dating-related stress, 24

discussion, 25-27
individual and social factors in, 25
literature review, 18-20
results, 22-25
study design, 20-22
Daughters of Bilitis, 33
Dependency, partner violence and,
125-126
Developmental context, of adolescent
passionate friendship, 10-11
Developmental issues, in dating and
courtship, 89-91
Domestic violence, 121-127. *See also*
Partner violence
Dress and grooming, 33
Dress behaviors, 33. *See also*
Physical appearance
Duration, of relationships, 53-63. *See
also* Stability of
relationships

Eating disorders, 34

Flirtation behaviors, 2
Florida International University,
85-109
Friendships
cross-generational, 139-148. *See
also* Cross-generational
friendships
with heterosexual women,
149-161. *See also*
Lesbian/heterosexual
friendships
intimate in adolescents, 5-16. *See
also* Adolescent friendships
lesbian in general, 140-142
research on, 150-151
types of, 143

Friendship script, 89,94-95. *See also*
Passionate friendship
Friendship vs. romance. *See also*
Passionate friendship
in lesbian dating and courtship,
100-103
Gender assignment, 76-77
Gender roles, 75-84
in dating and courtship, 88-89,103-104
Goldfarb Fear of Fat Scale, 35
Grooming and dress, 33
Group membership, physical appearance
and, 31-43

Heterosexist bias, 2
Heterosexual privilege, 159
Homophobia, as issue in couples
therapy, 131-132

Intimacy, as issue in couples therapy,
132-136

John Jay College-CUNY, 111-119

Lesbian battering, 121-127. *See also*
Partner violence
"Lesbian bed death," 111-119
compared with heterosexual, 114-115
literature review, 112-113
personal experiences, 116-118
sexual script flexibility and, 115-116
Lesbian/heterosexual friendships,
149-161
conclusion, 160
literature review, 150-151
method, 151-152
negative themes of, 157-160
positive themes of, 152-157
results and discussion, 152-160

Marriage, 82-83,94
  relationship stability and, 60-61
Merger, as issue in couples therapy,
  132-136
Midlife, dating and courtship in,
  85-109. *See also* Dating and
  Courtship
Minnesota State University, 45-51
(University of) Missouri-St. Louis,
  31-43
Mothers, relationships with, 83-84
My Life as a Boy (Chernin), 79-80
Myths, about lesbian battering,
  123-124

Nonverbal behaviors, 33-34

Ohio State University, 75-84
Pacific University, 129-138
Partner violence, 121-127
  as compared with heterosexual,
    123
  dynamics of lesbian battering,
    124-126
  interventions, 126-127
  myths about lesbian, 123-124
  rates of victimization, 122-124
Passionate friendships, in
    adolescents, 5-16. *See also*
    Adolescent friendships
(University of) Pennsylvania,
  139-148
Permanence, of relationships, 53-63
Personal advertisements, 45-51
Physical appearance, group
    membership and, 31-43

Racism, African American lesbian
    relationships and, 65-74

Relationship commitment, 53-63
Relationships, duration of, 53-63. *See
    also* Stability of relationships
Risk factors, in dating experience, 26
Romance script, 94,95-96. *See also*
    Passionate friendship
Rusbult's model of commitment and
    stability, 58-59

Scripts. *See also* Passionate friendship
  dating and courtship, 86-88,93-96
  flexibility of sexual, 115-116
  friendship, 89,94-95
  heterosexual vs. lesbian courtship,
    88-89
  romance, 94,95-96
  sexually explicit, 96
Seduction, 102-103
Self-esteem, dating experience and, 25
Sexual behavior, 111-119
  as compared with gays and
    homosexuals, 132-133
  as compared with heterosexual,
    114-115
  literature review, 112-113
  personal experiences, 116-118
  sexual script flexibility and, 115-116
Sexual identity, adolescent passionate
    friendship and, 13-14
Sexually explicit script, 96. *See also*
    Passionate friendship
Sexual signaling, 31-43
Social class
  African American lesbian
    relationships and, 65-74
  African American values and, 69-70
  case studies, 70-72
  legacy of, 66-69
Societal benefits, of lesbian/heterosexual
    friendships, 156
Societal stressors, on
    lesbian/heterosexual
    friendships, 159
St. John's University, 65-74

Stability of relationships, 53-63
Stigmatization, relationship stability
    and, 60
Stress, relationship stability and, 60
Substance abuse, partner violence and,
    125

Therapy, couples, 129-138. *See also*
    Couples therapy

Uniqueness, in lesbian dating and
    courtship, 97-100
University of California-Los Angeles,
    53-63
University of Missouri-St. Louis,
    31-43

University of Pennsylvania, 139-148
University of Utah, 5-16
University of Vermont, 149-161
University of Washington-Tacoma,
    121-127

Violence, partner, 121-127. *See also*
    Partner violence

Washington University, 17-29

Young adulthood, dating and courtship
    in, 85-109. *See also* Dating
    and Courtship